Towards a United States of Europe

TOWARDS A
UNITED STATES
OF EUROPE

*An analysis of Britain's role
in European Union*

R. W. G. MACKAY

With a preface by
PAUL-HENRI SPAAK

GREENWOOD PRESS, PUBLISHERS
WESTPORT, CONNECTICUT

Library of Congress Cataloging in Publication Data

Mackay, Ronald William Gordon, 1902-
    Towards a United States of Europe.

    Reprint of the ed. published by Hutchinson, London.
    Bibliography: p.
    Includes index.
    1. European federation. 2. European Economic
Community--Great Britain. 3. Great Britain--Relations (general) with Europe. 4. Europe--Relations (general) with Great Britain. I. Title.
D1060.M28   1976   301.29'41'04   75-31435
ISBN 0-8371-8509-2

First published in 1961 by Hutchinson, London

Reprinted with the permission of Hutchinson Publishing Group, Ltd.

Reprinted in 1976 by Greenwood Press,
a division of Williamhouse-Regency Inc.

Library of Congress Catalog Card Number 75-31435

ISBN 0-8371-8509-2

Printed in the United States of America

For

D.M.M., M.A.M., and C.S.M.

in the hope that they will
see a united Europe established
in their lifetime

PUBLISHER'S NOTE

R. W. G. Mackay died while *The Third Europe* was in production. Due to a variety of reasons it was decided to publish *Towards a United States of Europe*, although part of the larger work, on its own. The publishers particularly wish to thank John Pinder for invaluable help and advice and all those others who have so generously contributed in various ways.

ACKNOWLEDGMENTS

Grateful thanks are extended to the following authors and publishers for permission to quote from their works: the late Aneurin Bevan and William Heinemann Ltd., *In Place of Fear*; Rt. Hon. C. R. Attlee and William Heinemann Ltd., *As It Happened*; Dr. A. H. Robertson and Stevens and Sons, *European Institutions*; Sir Winston Churchill and Cassell and Co. Ltd., *The Sinews of Peace*; Professor R. H. Tawney and Allen & Unwin Ltd., *Equality*; Professor R. H. Tawney and S.C.M. Press Ltd., *The Western Political Tradition*; Dr. Arnold J. Toynbee and Oxford University Press, *The World after the Peace Conference* and *Civilization on Trial*; Sir Keith Hancock and Oxford University Press, *Survey of British Commonwealth Affairs*; Lord Lothian and Oxford University Press, *Pacifism Is Not Enough*; Sir John Wheeler-Bennett and Macmillan & Co. Ltd., *The Nemesis of Power*; Judge William O. Douglas and Victor Gollancz Ltd., *Strange Lands and Friendly People*.

Towards a United States of Europe

An analysis of Britain's role
in European Union

'I represent a party which does not yet exist: Civilization. This party will make the twentieth century. There will issue from it, first, the United States of Europe, and then the United States of the World.'

VICTOR HUGO

These words were found scrawled on a piece of paper among Victor Hugo's manuscripts and in memory of him were written on the wall of the room in Paris where he died in 1885.

'Nationality does not aim either at liberty or prosperity, both of which it sacrifices to the imperative necessity of making the nation the mould and measure of the State. Its course will be marked with material as well as moral ruin.'

ACTON (1862), *Lectures on Modern History*

'What confronts us today is not merely the old story of the rivalries of ambitious nations, or the too familiar struggles of discordant economic interests. It is the collapse of two great structures of thought and government, which for long held men's allegiance, but which now have broken down. The first is the system of independent national states, each claiming full sovereignty as against every other. The second is an economic system which takes as its premise that every group and individual shall be free to grab what they can get, and hold what they can grab. Those methods of organizing the affairs of mankind may be admired or detested, but two facts are incontestable. In the past they worked, though with endless waste and ill will; they now work no longer. The result is the anarchy, international and economic, which threatens to overwhelm us.'

R. H. TAWNEY, *Equality*

'There must be recognition of an international authority superior to the individual States and endowed not only with rights over them but with power to make them effective, operating not only in the political but the economic sphere. Europe must federate or perish.'

C. R. ATTLEE, *Labour's Peace Aims*

'The outstanding lesson of this second world war is that there can be no security for nations against aggression, no security for individuals against poverty, no protection for the growth of democracy and freedom, unless the keys of economic power, the essential means of production, are brought under public ownership or control, and unless military power is brought under effective control by a political authority of world-wide scope. Unless victory leads to a new assurance of peace, prosperity and democratic liberty, we shall have lost the peace; and without a wide extension of Socialist principle and a limitation of national sovereignty, that assurance will be impossible. Civilization will not escape yet another such disaster unless this war results in victory for our Socialist and internationalist cause. This is a conflict of principles, and Labour will strive with might and main to ensure that the right cause will win.'

REPORT OF THE NATIONAL EXECUTIVE COMMITTEE OF THE LABOUR PARTY, 1942–3

'A horrible retrogression back to the Middle Ages, without their chivalry, without their faith. Yet all this could be ended in a single stroke. Two or three hundred millions of people in Europe have only got to wake up one morning and resolve to be happy and free by becoming one family of nations, banded together from the Atlantic to the Black Sea for mutual aid and protection. One spasm of resolve! One single gesture!'

WINSTON CHURCHILL, 1946

'An integration of Europe, whatever its precise form, which broadened the basis of her economy, eliminated customs barriers and competing currencies, and enabled the basic industries of food, fuel, iron and steel, and engineering to be organized to serve a market of two hundred million persons, would unquestionably be followed by a general increase in economic prosperity and political strength; but the particular sacrifices and temporary embarrassments entailed by it would not be a trifle. Reason is on its side; but the natural human egotisms of interest and emotion; of loyalty, class and occupation; of regional loyalties and national pride, will rally to resist it.'

PROFESSOR R. H. TAWNEY, *The Western Political Tradition*

'The national sovereignties that we have all come to take for granted may prove to have been a luxury in which the people of western Christendom, overseas and in Europe, have been able to indulge a brief "Modern age" —now ancient history—in which we were enjoying an exceptional spell of freedom from external pressure. At any rate, today we are once again engaged in the usual struggle for the preservation of our western way of life. The freedoms in which this consists are applications of Christian principles, and national sovereignty is not one of these. If the peoples of western Christendom do not subordinate their national sovereignties now with one accord, we may lose the cold war. Our choice may lie between winning the cold war by subordinating national sovereignties and forfeiting national sovereignties by losing the cold war. We members of the western community who are citizens of the United Kingdom might be wise to take to heart Cleanthe's admission to God and destiny: "And if I wince and rebel, I know I shall have to follow your marching orders just the same." '

PROFESSOR ARNOLD TOYNBEE, Letter to the London *Times*, June 1950

Contents

Author's Note

The title to this book, *The Third Europe*,* needs some explanation. The first Europe lasted about four centuries, from A.D. 800 to 1200; the second from about A.D. 1200 to the beginning of this century. We are now in the throes of working out the form of the third Europe, and this book is an attempt to describe that form and to show how the third Europe could and should be created.

The first Europe—which is the title given by Mr. Delisle Burns to his famous work on the subject—dates from the Middle Ages, and was a Europe of United Christendom. Although the local lords were in continuous minor conflict, there was a unity of Western Christendom which, in effect, brought about the unity of Europe. It dates roughly from the time of Charlemagne in A.D. 8oo, for its creation took almost four centuries after the decline and fall of the Roman Empire.

The second Europe came into existence at the Renaissance and the Reformation, and it has lasted until the twentieth century. It was a Europe of independent sovereign states always reducing in number by the formation of larger nation states such as France, Italy, Germany and the United Kingdom. In the seventeenth, eighteenth and nineteenth centuries these independent states saved themselves from extermination in mutual conflict only by expansion overseas. They sent both man-power and capital to North and South America, to India, China, Australia, New Zealand and Africa. Expansion on such a large scale has now ended, and the two world wars, 1914–18 and 1939–45, plus the period of economic instability before and after the Second World War, both serve to show that the second Europe is in process of disintegration.

Will there be a third Europe? That is the question for the present generation of Europeans to determine for themselves. Will Europe undergo some kind of transformation of a political nature in the second half of the twentieth century which will preserve both its unity and its identity? This book is an attempt to answer those questions, and to show how a political union of Western Europe with Britain as a full partner could be created, the process of disintegration retarded, and the transformation brought about.

The detailed argument of the book can be summarized in a few sentences:

* This book was originally intended to be one Part, entitled *The Third Europe*, of a larger volume, the whole of which would have had the same title.

Firstly, that any citizen who wishes to see democracy survive can serve his generation best by promoting continental or regional democratic federations so as to create the smallest number of effective political authorities with limited functions but real powers over the largest areas, and comprising as large a number of people as possible, as a step in the direction of ultimate democratic world federal government.

Secondly, that the process of creating effective regional political authorities should begin in Western Europe.

Thirdly, that Britain has a very important role to play in joining in the creation of a European Union, or a United States of Europe, so that the gap which exists between the Common Market Six and the seven countries of E.F.T.A. shall be properly bridged.

Fourthly, that there is no reason why Britain should not join the Common Market forthwith, and why it should not then make suitable arrangements with the Commonwealth countries to the mutual advantage of both the Commonwealth and Europe.

Fifthly, that it will be fatal for Britain, and for Europe, if Britain should avoid her responsibilities in Western Europe on the grounds of her association with the Commonwealth, or the United States, for arguments on those lines are merely red herrings.

Sixthly, that the survival of Britain depends more on the success with which she adjusts herself to the world-wide revolutionary changes which affect her, than to her own domestic economic problems. For the solution of those problems will be conditioned more by the international climate than by the weather at home.

There is nothing original in this book. I have drawn considerably on the thought and writings of others. I am grateful for the help I have received, often quite unwittingly, from many of my former parliamentary colleagues, and from the discussions with my many friends in the parliaments of Europe and the other side of the Atlantic, and from my attendances both at the House of Commons and at the Council of Europe in Strasbourg. Noël Salter, the Clerk Assistant of the Assembly of W.E.U., my secretary at Strasbourg in 1949, and constant friend and collaborator since then, has always been of enormous help. I should like to take this opportunity of thanking those who have helped in the preparation of the manuscript, Violet Findlay and Joan Elphinstone, and, above all, my secretary over the last eight years, Barbara Blythe, to whom I owe a real debt of gratitude for valuable assistance during that time. But to two people I wish to express my special gratitude: to my sister Sheila, who has always been willing to read and criticize anything I have written, and to my wife Doreen, who has given me considerable assistance in a number of different ways on so many occasions, and I only hope she realizes just how very grateful I am.

Preface

In writing the preface to this posthumous work of R. W. G. Mackay I do not want only to introduce to the public a good book; I want also to render affectionate homage to a man for whom I had as much esteem as friendship.

It is a strange intellectual destiny, the destiny of this Australian, who came and settled in Great Britain and who was to be one of the most resolute champions for a United Europe.

I saw much of him during the first years, the heroic years of the Council of Europe. He brought to the work of the new Organization not only profound knowledge of economic problems and an exceptional wealth of learning, but also the warmth of moving conviction.

In the first Consultative Assembly, so rich in brilliant personalities and so full of hopes and ideals, he immediately came to the fore as one of the speakers to whom his colleagues listened with the closest attention. It was not possible to resist the combined charm of his courtesy of manner, his manifest knowledge and his active sincerity.

Those who in the future write the history of United Europe, and study the work of Strasbourg during the period 1949 to 1954, will find Mackay's constructive and zealous action everywhere. In all the great debates he was at the heart of the struggle, amongst those who wanted the most audacious and rapid progress. Alas, he was not always followed.

In the United Europe which he wished to see achieved, Great Britain naturally had her place. He therefore had to overcome not only the prudence of the countries of the Continent, but even more the reticence and apprehensions of his own.

He has not—he has not *yet*—succeeded. I say 'not yet' because the ideas which he has so generously sown, the efforts he made with so much perseverance and courage, will bear fruit—so I earnestly hope—in the near future.

He was a forerunner—with the enthusiasm which assured foresight gives, and the bitterness of failing to convince others.

His posthumous book, this cry, this appeal which sounds forth when his voice is silent for ever, has something pathetic about it. The man may be dead, but the idea which he cherished is not. He continues to fight for it.

This book, his last work, is published at a particularly opportune moment.

Great Britain, confronted with facts, must reconsider her European policy. The Common Market is a reality she can no longer ignore, after believing for so long that it would never be accomplished.

General de Gaulle is preparing to give a spectacular new impulse to the idea of political Europe. We cannot, nor do we wish to, reply negatively to his call: but our nostalgia and even our anxiety at having to go forward without Great Britain along the path which is proposed, are very great and very real.

The hour of the last chance is going to sound. In a speech delivered recently in the House of Lords, Lord Boothby recalled rightly that, immediately after the war, if Great Britain had so wished, it would have been easy for her to take the lead in a United Europe. Today this position of sole leader would probably be questioned. But a United Europe in which she would have her rightful place, in which she would have enormous influence, and where the other countries would be happy to benefit from her immense experience in international affairs, is still, and continues to be, possible. Tomorrow—a tomorrow which is not very far off—it will, no doubt, be too late. A continental Europe will form itself and follow its destiny, without having forged with the United Kingdom the links which to many of us appear so necessary.

This little Europe, let us repeat once more, we neither wanted nor desired. We have been driven to it by Great Britain's persistent refusal. We know perfectly well that this political construction is incomplete, and we realize how much of our ideal has been amputated. We can only continue to hope that, with her traditional realism, Great Britain will understand in time the error she would make in refusing to associate herself with what will, no doubt, be the greatest political event of the second half of the twentieth century.

And if one day our hope is realized—if Great Britain makes the decision we are waiting for, if she joins with Europe, without, of course, giving up her place in the Commonwealth—then, on that day, men should have a thought of gratitude for R. W. G. Mackay, the tenacious fighter; the forerunner, heard at last, and victorious.

P. H. SPAAK

CHAPTER 1

Britain at the Crossroads

*'If we could first know where we are and whither we are
tending, we could better judge what to do and how to do it.'*

Abraham Lincoln

THE British people are at the crossroads. Important decisions of a
political nature must be made before they move forward. Revolutionary changes have been made during this century in Britain's
external position. Their nature and extent have not been fully appreciated
either by the public or the parties conducting government since the end
of the First World War. These changes affect military, political, economic,
commonwealth and colonial policies. All need to be adjusted to the changing world. The aeroplane, atomic energy, hydrogen bombs and nuclear
weapons, the development of mass production and automation, the
emergence of millions of people from their shackles of political servitude
in several countries have ushered in a new age. A new science of politics
is wanted, one as different from the world of the sixteenth century in which
the modern national state took shape as nuclear weapons are from
muzzle-loading firearms. The world community which then comprised
only the continent of Europe today extends all over the globe and comprises some 2,795 million people, in 123 different countries, and ten continental regions, which differ considerably in their ideologies, their political
systems, their regions, their standards of living and their productive
capacity. In these changed conditions what does the future hold for the
people of the United Kingdom in Britain? And what shall Britain's reac-
tion be to this very different world?

If we are at the crossroads then we must look for the signposts: and
decide by which road to proceed on our journey, or otherwise muddle along
like a horse in blinkers not knowing what choice to make. There are many
signposts and many groups of people who will each suggest a different
course. Do we go it alone, as in the past, relying on our power and
prestige to maintain the position of a great power which we held for so
long but which is a position which we can hardly maintain today? Do we

try to create a strong but larger political entity such as the Common-wealth—a European Union—or a North Atlantic Alliance, thereby sur-rendering much of our sovereignty and certainly our position as an individual power but perhaps achieving a greater measure of security? Or do we rely on the United Nations and the unity of the great powers and endeavour to keep up with the position of one of the great powers which we held prior to the First World War?.

(i) Great Power Unity, Security and Western Defence

Britain ended the Second World War with a feeling of confidence in the future. The peace of the world would be maintained by the unity of the three great powers, the United States, the Soviet Union and Great Britain, or—if we add France and China—by the unity of the five permanent mem-bers of the Security Council. The United Nations Charter was accepted; the Security Council and the Assembly were created; the conception of great-power unity was embodied in the voting provisions of the Security Council of the United Nations. With a Labour Government in power in Britain it was hoped back in 1945 in Mr. Bevin's words that 'Left would under-stand Left'; that Britain would act as a bridge between the Soviet Union and the United States; and that with such a link peace would be main-tained. Thus with the creation of a form of collective security it was believed by many that another world war would never break out; that a world-police system would be established; that disputes between all nations great and small would be settled by the Security Council; and that con-siderable reductions could be made in defence expenditure. Fortified by these beliefs, the United States and Britain took steps after 1945 to reduce their armaments.

Disillusionment soon set in. The Soviet Union emerged from the war as a country strongly aggressive, nationalist, isolated and imperialistic, so that, in world affairs, this Communist country assumes an aspect which is more imperialistic and menacing that the Russia of Czarist days. She has embarked on a policy of territorial expansion, spilling over into the power vacuum which was left in Central and Eastern Europe by Germany's defeat. Within a few years after the end of the war, she had brought within her control three Baltic states, Rumania, Bulgaria, Yugoslavia, Hungary, Poland, Albania, Eastern Germany and Czechoslovakia. This expansion gave rise to suspicions on the part of the West which the attitude of the Soviet Union towards the United States and vice versa did little to remove. Both countries seemed to be encircling the other. The Soviet Union has used its veto in the Security Council on eighty-four occasions (July 1958) and so, in effect, has made that body powerless to act. Had the representative of the Soviet Union been present when the decision to intervene in Korea was taken, the Security Council could not have acted at all. Thus the powers, having ceased to rely on the Security Council as an instrument where decisions can be made and action taken, turned to the Assembly, only to find that little progress could be made; and for a very good reason as the world was not one world but two. For, if the United Nations were to function successfully as a world authority, it was essential that the wartime unity of the great powers should continue into and throughout the peace. Unfortunately, that condition has never been in operation. The Iron Curtain has become a reality; and the peoples of the Soviet Union and its satellites and the United States and her Western Allies are divided into what seems for the time being two irreconcilable groups. But as the division between the Soviet Union and the West was making itself felt and the great-power unity was being recognized as nonexistent, other changes were taking place in the power basis of international relationships.

In China, the Communists succeeded in overthrowing the nationalist régime of Chiang Kai-Shek with the result that the barrier between the West and the Soviet Union was further extended. China, an ally in both world wars, became separated from the West. Moreover, the forces of nationalism in South East Asia, the Middle East and Africa were bringing to the fore with an unprecedented impact, in addition to claims for independence, the whole question of colour and race conflict and, in this conflict, the nationalist movements were supported by the Soviet Union, while Western Europe with its imperialistic traditions and bad record in parts of Africa and South East Asia was at a grave disadvantage. Finally, Germany and Japan were re-emerging as very powerful nations in competition with many of their wartime opponents. Thus a new policy was needed, which would serve not only as a substitute for great-power unity, but would be adequate to satisfy these other new factors of the situation as well.

The first half of the twentieth century witnessed: the two greatest wars the world has known; a revolution in Russia and a Russian famine; thirty years' revolutionary war in China; and the political awakening of nearly one-half of the world's population—the people of Asia and Africa. Today millions of people are on the march following creeds that are irreconcilable and shouting slogans that are in conflict with one another. Nor are the differences between them of little importance. They are differences of religion, of economic theories, of political faiths, of race and of colour. Thus in a situation charged with so much explosive matter, while we may hope to survive, we can hardly look forward to having an easy journey through the second half of the twentieth century. Today it is not so difficult to enumerate the places where there is both conflict and instability.

In the Far East: in Korea, Formosa, Indo-China and Tibet. In India: the uneasy peace in Kashmir and the suspicious hostility between India and Pakistan. In the Middle East: the threat of trouble in Iraq; the legacy of mistrust between Britain and the United Arab Republic; the hostility of the Arabs to Israel; 'and the nationalist conflict between the Arabs themselves. In Africa: racial trouble in the south; conflict with Britain over the protectorates; trouble in the Central African Federation; constitutional conflict in Uganda and Kenya; French conflict in Algeria; and the ever present racial hostility and national upheaval throughout the whole continent. In Europe: the division of Berlin and of Germany; the building up of armed forces in Western Europe under the auspices of N.A.T.O. with American pressure and aid; the presence of large numbers of Russian troops in the satellite countries; and the domination by the Soviet Union of at least eighty million Europeans. These are some of the events and happenings in the first decade after the Second World War which will be noted by the historian in A.D. 2000.

The period is one marked by a struggle for power between the forces of Communism, headed by the Politburo in Moscow, and the forces of free peoples of the world under the leadership of the United States Administration in Washington. Force is being met with force. The world is divided into two camps; totalitarian and free; Communists and democrats; Russians and anti-Russians; Americans and anti-Americans, according to the continent from which one views the preparations for the struggle, with a large number of neutral countries observing the struggle from the side-lines before deciding which side to join. The various conflicts throughout the world can be understood only as part of this main conflict, and one wonders: what will be the outcome of the drive for national independence, not only by the Indians and the Chinese and those others who have it, but by those peoples in Africa and elsewhere who are still struggling to win it? Will the peoples of South East Asia, of Africa and the Arab world join forces with the West or with the Soviet Union?

We must, therefore, be realistic about the position which faces us in Britain and the Western world in its search for peace and security. World government, however desirable, is premature. Collective security for the world based on the sovereign equality of national states is no substitute for government in international affairs. The United Nations, while it serves many useful purposes where the nations are willing to co-operate in social and cultural fields, does not provide the machinery for making the kind of political decisions that must be made if conflict between the great powers is to be avoided. For, as the last fifteen years have demonstrated to all but the blind and deaf, the differences between the freedom-loving peoples of the world (however much they may fall by the wayside in their practice of it) and the totalitarian régimes are fundamental. We are back where we were before the two world wars with a vengeance, with a world in two camps each armed more heavily than ever before and each professing conflicting ideas, principles and policies, thus creating a gap which it seems impossible to bridge.

(ii) *The Western Alliance*

Faced with the breakdown of great-power unity and the division of the world into two blocs, some of the statesmen of the free world in Western Europe have turned to the better organization of Western Europe, or to the creation of the Atlantic Alliance, so as to ensure that they have the effective support of the United States, not half-way through the next war (as on the last two occasions), but in the period of the armed peace, and before war breaks out.

An Atlantic community has many obvious attractions, and may serve to prevent war breaking out, but the differences between the members—some of which are substantial and, perhaps, fundamental—are rarely brought out in the open and squarely faced, at least by the countries of Western Europe. If it means anything, the Atlantic Alliance means a partnership in which one partner in wealth and power, the United States, dominates all the rest of the partners taken together. It means, too, the rearmament of Germany, for this is a term of the Alliance on which the United States insists, and in which Britain has acquiesced. And if the world is to be divided into two power blocs, one of which is led by the United States, then it means an expenditure in armaments which threatens the economic stability of the countries of Western Europe and particularly of Britain.

There are disagreements too between the partners of the free world. The Government of the United States does not see eye to eye with some of its associates in Western Europe over a number of questions. The general approach of the West to the Soviet Union, whether by compromise or not, is one. Whether Fascist Spain should be brought into the family is another. The recognition of Communist China and the inclusion of its representatives in the Security Council and the Assembly of the United Nations is a third. The future of Formosa is a fourth, and the union of the two Germanies a fifth. The position of France in the Alliance, her Algerian policy and refusal to accept on her territory American atomic weapons, is a sixth. The rearmament of Germany, and its inclusion in the North Atlantic Treaty Organization, though agreed to by the N.A.T.O. powers, has unsettled the relations between France, Britain and the United States for several years, and a common policy for the future development of Europe—outstanding since 1945—has yet to be agreed between those three powers. And there are many more questions yet to be resolved.

Differences, too, exist between the United States and Great Britain over trade policies; and between the peoples of both countries and of some European countries arising out of the conflict between the welfare state and Socialism on the one hand, and free enterprise and competition on the other. These differences should not be unexpected or resented. There will always be conflicts between democratic peoples of any community in the period of their growth, and those conflicts will be magnified or exaggerated when, as it happens in the case of Europe and the United States, the people live many miles apart in separate countries and continents and have their own particular attitude towards the problem of social change. The newer countries of North America have reacted differently from the states of Western Europe to the awakening of the peoples of Africa and Asia, and the divergencies in their respective responses to these problems widens the gap between the political thinking in the two continents and makes common action between them almost impossible.

If there are differences between the countries of the so-called free world as such, there are also differences of a substantial nature between the citizens of the individual countries. People refer to Britain as a Socialist, or to the United States as a capitalist country, but such designations are quite inaccurate and fail to recognize the substantial differences of opinion that exist in each country over such questions. For, in fact, no such generalization should be made about any nation or the people of any state in the Western group of nations. In Britain, whatever political differences existed during the war on domestic matters, the gaps between the parties were closed and a united effort was made by the nation to defeat Hitler. In 1945 the wartime Coalition came to an end. The parties split into open opposition over domestic issues, though for a period of nearly ten years they accepted a bi-partisan policy for foreign affairs and defence. While there may have been differences in emphasis or in degree, it did not matter whether Mr. Bevin, Mr. Morrison, Mr. Eden or Mr. Macmillan were at the Foreign Office, or Mr. Strachey, Mr. Head or Mr. Duncan Sandys at the War Office. Whoever was the chief and whatever his party, Britain's policy in foreign affairs and defence remained virtually the same. What was true of Britain in those post-war years is equally true of the United States; for during the Truman administration, and until the death of Senators Vandenberg and Taft, the United States has followed a bi-partisan foreign policy for approximately fifteen years. But there were differences of opinion in each of the parties in both countries over the policies followed and these differences have become more and more marked over the last few years. Today the two main parties in Britain are opposed to one another on both foreign affairs and defence policy and the same may shortly be true of the parties on the other side of the Atlantic. For with the passing of the years and the conversion of the cold war into a cold peace, differences which cut openly across party lines (but which had remained quietly below the surface) have now been brought more and more into the open.

Thus there are struggles at three levels: the struggle for world power between the two power blocs—epitomized as the 'cold war'; the conflict between the countries which comprise the two opposing groups in the world; and the differences between the political parties in the individual countries of each group. And we do little service to an adequate discussion of Britain's place in the modern world unless all of these many differences are frankly recognized and freely discussed.

(iii) The German Problem

The conception of Western defence, though based on a coalition of the powers of Western Europe and of North America, raises the whole question of the future of Western Germany and its association both with the West and with North America. The integration of Western Germany has been fundamental to the development of the conception for Western defence for it is considered that German people, German industrial resources and German skill are all required for the adequate defence of Western Europe. For, if a democratic Germany could be united and brought into the Western European security system, Western Europe could be strong enough to prevent a Russian attack.

This proposal, of course, raises a number of difficult problems: the genuine fear which many have over the rearmament of Western Germany; the former rivalry between Western Germany and France; and the political aspect of Western Germany's association either with Western Europe or with the North Atlantic Treaty Organization. For the concept of Western defence involves gathering Western Germany into Western Europe, identifying her interests entirely with those of the Western European powers and integrating her military potential with that of the other countries of Western Europe, including Britain. It was this concept which led to the development of the European Defence Community and the treaty to create it, which owing chiefly to objections by France but also to those from British and German Socialists has now been quietly buried. But German rearmament proceeds apace even though it still remains a controversial subject both in the West and with the East. Perhaps no bigger issue divides the countries today on both sides of the Iron Curtain; nor is this division difficult to understand. Twice in our lifetime the Germans, dominated by their military imperialists, have overrun Europe, West and

East. Although they were ultimately driven back, they inflicted immense suffering and indignities on the peoples and the lands which they invaded. On both occasions the conduct of the German armies showed the contempt of the German ruling and military class for international law and civilized human behaviour. In the Second World War, when the army was under control of the Nazis, we saw mass murder, destruction and brutality of a kind unknown in any previous century.

In his *The Nemesis of Power* Sir John Wheeler-Bennett quotes two very prophetic dicta about the Prussians recorded by Mirabeau in 1788: 'Prussia is not a country which has an army, it is an army which has a country. War is the national industry of Prussia.' And Wheeler-Bennett continues:

> No country has been so roundly and truly defeated as Prussia at Jena and Germany at the close of the First and Second World Wars. No country has displayed a more phenomenal capacity for military resilience or for beating ploughshares into swords. On the occasions of each of these pronounced ˎefeats, the victor sought by every means and device known in his age, by restrictions and supervision and compulsion, to destroy the German potential for war, physically, morally, and spiritually. All three attempts were to prove futile. . . . In each case the victors were outwitted to their subsequent detriment.[1]

But, as Wheeler-Bennett points out, we should be doing less than our duty and even a positive disservice to posterity if, in our anxiety to secure the future, we would forget or ignore the lessons of the past. For the army had the responsibility for bringing the Nazis to power, for tolerating the infamies of that régime once it had attained power, and for not removing the régime from power; and one cannot help asking, will it not happen again? Against such background, we have to review the question of German rearmament. Can we suppose the indoctrination of youth by the Nazis has left behind no legacy? Will not a rearmed Germany set out to regain its old imperial power? Will it not in default of agreement over a united Germany make war to win back its lost provinces or even seek compensation for its losses in the West?

These questions raise very important considerations but there is one other which we forget at our peril—namely the futility of any attempt to keep Germany neutral. Every possible step was taken to secure that result in 1919. We are confronted with the stark reality that, whether we like it or not, Western Germany has regained her sovereignty, and is in the process of rearming. What confronts us is not the question whether they should be allowed to rearm, but, how can this rearmament take place in a framework strong enough to prevent a recurrence of the militarism that we have known in the past?*

* The W.E.U. Agency for the control of Armaments, established by the Paris Agreements in October 1954, does not meet this requirement.

The answer to this question can only be found in the creation of a European Political Community to which Germany like other states surrenders a substantial part of her sovereignty. The Atlantic community or N.A.T.O. offers no such solution. The way to insure against the revival of German militarism is to see that Germany no longer is a sovereign state in the sense that she and France and Britain were prior to the Second World War. By that means, and by that means only, can we guarantee that she has no sovereign control over her foreign affairs, her rearmament or her defence. By creating a European Political Community and by developing a political authority of the type already envisaged for the coal, steel and defence communities, we would establish a political authority which could control the armaments and the foreign policy of all the states of Western Europe which form it. In this way we take away from the control of individual parliaments of the states of Western Europe, foreign policy and defence, as these powers would be merged in the general powers of the political authority. For, as Mr. R. H. S. Crossman, M.P., pointed out in a broadcast some ten years ago:

The only way to solve the German problem is to create a political union of Western Europe of which Germany is a part and to impose permanently on the Germans only those sacrifices of sovereignty which we are prepared to impose on ourselves. We see, therefore, that the solution of the German problem is to be found not in Germany but in Paris and Brussels and London. Belgian and French statesmen are pressing for a European Assembly as the first stage in the advance to federal union. British statesmen are arguing for a functional approach which avoids directly tackling the fundamental political problem.[2]

Any policy of neutralism is illusory. We cannot avoid German rearmament in some form but we can and must avoid the creation of a German state in Western Europe with full sovereign powers over defence. The creation of a European Political Community with proper parliamentary institutions in which the Germans, French and British play a part is a real and practical approach to the solution to this problem. It will create a European army in which there will be German contingents, but they will be under the control, not of the military staff of Germany, but of a European Minister of Defence and of a parliament in Europe.

Some people will argue that if German rearmament is permitted the armaments will be used by the Germans in a war either against the Soviet Union, for German unification, or should that prove unobtainable, in a war against the West to secure compensation for the territory which Germany lost in the East. This argument has little to commend it. It is contrary to all the declarations of responsible politicians and of all the major parties in Germany. It could apply only (if at all) if German armaments were to proceed outside the European Political Community.

The creation of a European community with such German forces as exist forming a part of it would make it impossible for the Germans to use their arms to force any war; for any such war would require the agreement of all the members of the community.

It would be wrong to suppose that the only question at issue is the one of German rearmament based on a fear of a recurrence of German militarism. The complex problem is the unity of Germany, the hostility of the Soviet Union to any rearmament of Western Germany, and the failure of the Foreign Ministers to agree upon a common policy with regard to the unification of Germany. Here again, many people are apt to follow illusions. Germany can be united either by force or by agreement. Force almost inevitably would involve war with the Russians, which none of the countries of the West would be prepared to commence, and of which the outcome would, in any event, be doubtful. So as a method of unification it can be ruled out.

We are left, therefore, with agreement as the only possible method of uniting Germany, and this depends upon the willingness of the Soviet Union. Will they be ready to let the German people unite in a free state, leaving it to them to decide freely with whom the state will associate, and in what manner? Some people take the view that agreement could be obtained for a united Germany if the Western Foreign Ministers had been prepared to give up the North Atlantic Treaty Organization. Anyone who draws this conclusion cannot have read the White Paper on the earlier Geneva conference, which discloses that there was no evidence that the Russians were ready to let free elections be held in Germany as they feared the consequences. While the Ministers of the West are not prepared to give up the North Atlantic Treaty Organization, they are willing to allow a united Germany to decide freely what group she wants to join, if any. To insist on the disbandment of N.A.T.O. or the Eastern bloc before a united Germany had been created would have been foolish; for the question of the rearmament of Germany is not really an obstacle to the unity of Germany. The only obstacle to the unity of Germany today, apart from some of the West Germans who do not want it, is the Russians. They fear that a united Germany would join with the West, and that they would then be subject to attack from the whole of Western Europe. The ghosts of 1914 and 1941 still remain with them. They prefer Germany divided and weak (and in consequence Western Europe divided and weak), rather than united and strong. German unity rests in the hands of the Soviet Union today, and they are using it as a bargaining factor in order to determine other disputes in which they are involved. There is a wide gap between the views of the West and the views of the Soviet Union on the solution of the German problem.

(iv) Britain—a Great Power?

In the previous sections of this chapter we have raised the questions of our relations with other powers and of the problems which we must face with the revival of Germany. Where do we stand in all this? What policy should this country follow? There is a need for an agonizing re-appraisal of Britain's policy. For the first time this century we must take stock of our position in relation to the other countries in the world, some more, some less powerful than ourselves, and we must formulate a foreign policy which bears a real relation to our resources. We will examine the decline of Europe and the position of Britain in a changing world in the next chapter and we shall see that Britain no longer is a great power in the sense that she is able to pursue an independent policy today as she could, and did, in the nineteenth century. N.A.T.O. and our European commitments result from our dependence and not our independence, or from our weakness and not our strength. This is particularly true in the field of defence for, as modern weapons have developed, we cannot provide for ourselves adequately and even when they are provided for us in concert with others the general costs of our defence become a burden which bears very heavily on our resources.

If we are no longer a great power, what are the consequences of the change in status? Must we be the fifty-first state of the United States or join in a merger with the other states of Western Europe? Or should we maintain a neutral position like Denmark prior to the war or Switzerland throughout the century? Or should we endeavour to join in a firm union with some or all of the Commonwealth countries and, if so, which? Finally, can an Atlantic union be made into a reality which could speak with one voice through one political authority? All these present avenues need to be explored. The consideration of these questions determines our choice of signposts and must determine the way we should go. But certain things emerge fairly clearly. For us colonialism or imperialism or the expansion of Britain is over; there must be no more Boston Tea Parties; Boer Wars; Suez madnesses; or events such as we saw in India before 1949 and in Cyprus in recent years. That phase of our history is finished. This means in our re-appraisal a reconsideration of our place in the world and in our relationship with other countries. We have been trying to carry out a foreign policy which smacks of Palmerston and the nineteenth century, with a rearmament programme greater than ever before and a domestic policy of expanded social reform. We cannot pursue all these policies at the same time. They are quite incompatible though both political parties have yet to realize much less to acknowledge this simple fact.

It is against this background that we must try to find out whither we

are tending. It is essential to face this question; can we carry out our
present external policy and a domestic programme of social reform at the
same time? Each of the parties is equally to blame for refusing to face
reality in considering this question. Like ostriches each one of them puts
its head in the sand and thinks that it cannot be seen. In its *Challenge
to Britain*, published in 1954, the Labour Party says that Britain's weakness
as a nation is her unwillingness to face the facts until the crisis is upon
her.[3] The crisis has been upon us now for over thirty-five years and neither
of the major political parties has faced it squarely at any time; nor does
either one recognize that we must resolve our external problems first,
before we can turn our attention to any programme of social improvement
on the home front. In their policy statement, the Labour Party asserts:
'There is still time to win the peace—on one condition—that we face the
hard facts of life and take the drastic Socialist measures which alone can
prevent catastrophe.' Then follows the plan which can alone prevent
catastrophe. It consists of thirty-three pages, of which twenty-eight are
devoted to the programme for expansion at home and the development
of the social services, and barely five to the question of our political and
economic security overseas. No attempt is made to formulate any effective
foreign policy which will make the adjustments necessary to meet the
revolutionary situation abroad. What is missing both from the Labour
Party's *Challenge to Britain*, and in so much political discussion today,
is any awareness that in the solution of Britain's problems, which are
many, the solution of external questions comes first. External problems
have led us into two wars in this century; to a series of economic crises
which now are becoming chronic; to the unemployment between the
wars; and to our present perilous position in which defence takes 7·5 per
cent of the national income—far more than the amount we spend on the
social services. The most drastic Socialist measures such as nationalization
of land, houses and public companies, without any compensation, and
the introduction of real and effective industrial self-government (neither
of which is the policy of the Labour Party, as yet), might serve to re-distri-
bute the wealth of the community (a good thing) but they would not resolve
any of the external problems outlined in this chapter, or make any contribution to our survival.

Considerations of this nature make controversial the Labour Party's
statement of policy, which argues that if fifty million people, crowded on
these islands, are to earn a decent living without relying on foreign aid
we must discard the prejudices and privileges of the past and plan the work
of our mines, our fields and our factories for the common good. One
wonders what contribution the planning of the work of our mines would
make to the solution of our external problems. It would not reduce the
cost of imported raw materials, nor would it reduce the cost of the food

which we have to import. In any event, the mines have been nationalized. The most that any planning can do now is to increase the production per man-hour, so adding to the amount of labour available for employment in other industries. We need something much more than planning of our mines, fields and factories. What we need is a large market, without any barriers, in which to sell the products of our factories. For a large market will lead to an increase in production per man-hour; to technological improvements; and to greater efficiency in industry. Here again we mistake the target. It may be true that the country has been encouraged by the Conservative Party to relax and dream of back to normal. What is more true is that the country has not been encouraged to realize that the solution of our political problems lies in giving attention to their external aspect, and that until we put these external problems first, with defence high on the agenda, we are not beginning to solve them.

This mistake in emphasis is a characteristic of the policy statement of the Labour Party. It begs the question as to whether survival means survival of this country amongst others, or whether it means survival of a way of life which was developed during the Labour Government in the post-war period. We are told by the Labour Party that the fight for survival went on even when Germany surrendered; that in the 'cold' as in the 'hot' war we had to struggle for our freedom; that since the Tories returned to power the country has been encouraged to relax, to dream back to normal; that their dream is vain for the way back is barred; that any attempt to restore free enterprise is impracticable; and that Socialism has become a necessity if we are to achieve security and the decent living standards that we desire. None of these considerations is relevant. For, unless we solve our external problems satisfactorily, none of the proposals contained in the *Challenge to Britain* will ever be put into effect. The *Challenge to Britain* advocates large-scale capital investment to increase production and exports, so that, without our continued dependence on the United States, we can provide for an improved welfare state. Such a plan is quite inconsistent with the proposals which are contained in the White Paper on defence. You could have either one or the other, but you cannot have both. Some of the Left Wing papers of the Labour Party realize this. They write that if the Opposition acquiesces in any long-term expenditure on the scale of the White Paper on defence it will be committing itself to a burden which makes nonsense of the promises contained in the *Challenge to Britain*.

We are involved in a struggle for power in the world, and our primary task is to determine our attitude towards that struggle, and the contribution which we can make to it. That task comes first. It may be that for many years our contribution to that struggle will absorb the whole of our political activities. We may have to postpone our expansion on the home front until we have produced stability abroad. There can be little doubt that if we had done this in 1919 we would be much further ahead in 1959 with our programme of social reform. Mr. Aneurin Bevan in his book *In Place of Fear* comes very near to recognizing the truth of this proposition. He writes:

> In the beginning of this book I spoke of political power and of how the problem of attaining it appeared to young workers like myself in the industrial towns and cities of Britain. We were preoccupied with how to raise the general standard of life. The pursuit of power presented itself to us in social and not in personal terms.[4]

This exactly expresses the point of view of the Labour Party today in its *Challenge to Britain*, and the views of many other people in all parties. They are preoccupied with how to raise the general standard of life in Great Britain. They think that the general standard of life can be raised in one country or in one part of the world quite regardless of the standards in other parts of the world. They think that in the second half of the twentieth century you can separate the 51·7 million people of Britain from the other 2,795 million people in the world, and create for them a standard of living which they can preserve for themselves and not share with their fellows. The history of the years covered by the two wars and the periods between them and since provides ample evidence of the postponement or defeat of proposals for social change, because governments have failed in the first instance to adjust themselves to the external conditions which were changing around them.

Mr. Bevan goes on:

> It is clearer to me now than it was then that the nation is too small an arena in which to hope to bring the struggle to a final conclusion. Thus the attainment of political power in the modern state still leaves many problems outside its scope. *National sovereignty is a phrase which history is emptying of meaning.*[5]

He sees that the nation is too small an arena in which to bring the struggle to a final conclusion, and that the attainment of political power by a party in any one modern state leaves many problems quite outside the competence of the party, however great its majority, for the problems and their solution are outside the competence of the individual national state. Yet, as we are beginning to see, these 'many problems' which are outside the scope of the state just happen to be the very problems which determine the conditions on which the state can survive. It follows, therefore, that these external problems must be tackled first; and that the expansion of the social services or the development of Socialism at home must be postponed until they have been tackled and satisfactorily disposed of. For it is these problems which happen to be the fundamental problems in the struggle for power between the forces on both sides of the Iron Curtain, and they take first place on our agenda, however much we may dislike it. And with the problem of defence expenditure they comprise such questions as our full participation in the economic and military life of Europe, the hiving off of our colonial burdens, the freeing of our colonial peoples, and the raising of the general standard of living of all peoples everywhere in the world. These questions determine the external situation on which our survival depends. It is difficult to see events in their proper perspective; but unless we solve these external problems of ours first we shall never have the opportunity to consider home affairs. Our economic survival must be secured before we can plan any improvement in our standard of living.

Thus we are faced with a fundamental decision. We must decide our policy on a number of international issues. We must carry out a plan which relates to foreign, colonial, economic and commonwealth affairs before we can contemplate a programme at home. We must solve our problem of external security before we can proceed further with the programme of social development. This brings us to the crossroads. What signposts do we follow? We will look at Europe and the Commonwealth as they appear in the second half of the twentieth century, and then consider what solution is offered Britain today.

CHAPTER 2

Britain in a Changing World

Abruptly Europe seemed to have reversed her rôle and to have changed from the focus of international affairs into a half-derelict continent.

Arnold J. Toynbee

Countries outside Soviet Russia are faced with a position for which there is no parallel at any rate since the days of the Roman Empire. Even the paramountcy of the United Kingdom in the final period of the industrial revolution, 1840 to 1860, was less complete than the present economic weight of the United States.

T. Balogh

A STUDY of the first fifty years of the twentieth century emphasizes a number of factors. The shrinkage in the political and economic strength of the states of Western Europe has been most marked. Despite a considerable increase in their production, world trade in manufactures has declined and Western Europe's share in both the production and trade of manufactures has diminished. The period of cheap raw materials and foodstuffs, on which in the past the prosperity of Western Europe largely depended, has now ended. Britain, dependent over several centuries for her prosperity on imports and exports, finds herself today faced with a completely different set of trading conditions in the world; for, with the development of economic nationalism, most states are endeavouring to make themselves economically self-sufficient. At the time when the decline of Western Europe has been taking place, North America has emerged as a giant economic force with the United States as a great world power and the Soviet Union has done likewise. As the United States and the Soviet Union have emerged to occupy the

34

only positions of great powers in the world, the relative position and strength of Western Europe have correspondingly declined.

It has been customary to look at this change in the prosperity of Europe as the aftermath of two world wars. But, while the destruction, waste and dislocation which resulted from those wars was vast, the evidence suggests that the problems of adjustment which confront the states of Western Europe today are not mainly due to the two world wars. Before the First World War the position of Western Europe in the world economy had weakened considerably. The world slump of 1929–31 revealed both the extent of the decline in Europe's economy and the disequilibrium which was then apparent between the old and the new worlds. By 1939 it was doubtful whether the most radical changes could save Western Europe from a major economic disaster though this was prevented or postponed by the outbreak of the Second World War.

(i) Europe's Decline in Relation to the New World

The first sixty years of the twentieth century have witnessed two world wars both followed, in 1919 and 1945, by periods of an armed peace. At the turn of the century six European powers, France, Germany, Italy, Austria-Hungary, Russia and Great Britain, and two outside Europe altogether, Japan and the United States, had together brought the greater part of the earth's surface, resources and population within their respective spheres of administration, control and influence. In the period before the First World War, these great powers dominated the stage, though 'their predominance would have been pronounced to be imposing rather than secure by most of the observers who looked below the surface and back into the past; for these leviathans were the creatures of two primary forces greater than themselves, which had brought them into existence blindly and unconsciously in one phase of their operation and had so entered upon another phase, in which they were beginning remorselessly to undo their work. These two forces were the industrial system and the principle of nationality.'[1] Of these eight great powers only two, one the Soviet Union partly inside Europe and the other the United States completely outside it, remain important today, though several countries, one of whom, India, did not exist as an independent country in 1914 and another, China, was not a part of the world-wide system of great powers in 1914, have emerged to such important positions as to take the place of those countries who have fallen to less important ones.

The sovereign states of Europe numbered sixteen in 1875, twenty-two in 1914, and twenty-five in 1959. Since the turn of the century they have increased by approximately 50 per cent. At the beginning of the twentieth century the industrial revolution had refashioned the framework of life in Western and Central Europe, but was still young and feeble in the agrarian East. Today the industrial revolution has made the Continent one; but while the economic development has gone one way, political development has gone another. The forces of nationalism have divided Europe. In doing so they have weakened the states of Europe. The forces of the industrial revolution which could have provided greater strength and stability for the peoples of Europe as a whole have not been permitted to give to Europe the benefits available. Interdependence has increased, but so also have the frontiers and with them economic barriers of all kinds.[2]

Nineteenth-century society was divided between the advanced industrial countries, mostly to be found amongst the great powers of Western Europe, and the backward, mostly colonial areas of Africa, Asia and the Middle East. This division of function, broadly corresponding with the division of colour, was the basis of the economy and the expansion of Western Europe. It was on this that the economic strength of the great powers of Western Europe rested. With the opening of the twentieth century this division was challenged. The stirrings of revolt against imperialism, or the domination of the Europeans, began to be felt. History records hardly one year in the twentieth century in which an attempt was not made by one or other of the backward peoples to secure some kind of independence, both political and economic. The Russian Revolution and Soviet propaganda, no doubt, have supported movements to this end. But they needed little external support. Japanese action in the Second World War probably brought the colonial revolution in Asia to a head and stimulated movements which have made it impossible to restore white supremacy in Asia, whether in a military, a political or an economic sense. All over the non-self-governing parts of the world there is a revolt against political, economic and racial inequality and dependency.

Naturally, these occurrences affected the states of Western Europe. Their colonies were taken from Germany in the First and from Italy in the Second World War. Some were parcelled out amongst the victors while others obtained their independence. The status of the remaining colonial territories of the other states of Western Europe has changed considerably since the beginning of the century. Eire is an independent republic outside the Commonwealth. Holland has given up control over Indonesia, which is now an independent republic. India, Ceylon, Burma and Malaya are now free and independent states like Eire, one not even a member of the Commonwealth. In Africa, Egypt, Tunisia, Morocco, the Sudan, Ghana, Nigeria, the Congo and most of French Africa have obtained independence. In 1900 most of the states of Western Europe drew part of their economic wealth and political power, and in some cases military forces, from their overseas territories. By the middle of the century some of these territories were independent, and others were in the process of becoming independent. In short, the colonial revolution was well started on its course.

The changed position in which the countries of Western Europe now find themselves must be attributed to a certain extent to the two world wars. Europe lost men and materials, suffered much devastation and enormous economic and political upheaval. Before the First World War Western Europe imported foodstuffs and raw materials from the rest of the world and exported manufactures and migrants. The balance of this immense traffic had been so favourable to her that she had been able to increase her standard of living and her population, and at the same time to save a margin of her profit from year to year for world investment. But this extraordinary prosperity, indeed the whole of her economic life, depended upon the regular working of an economic organization which was like an elaborate and delicate piece of machinery. The two world wars destroyed the working of this organization.

In the nineteenth century the Western European countries, and particularly the United Kingdom, secured the trade of the world because a quick start in the industrial revolution gave them a lead. They required raw materials and foodstuffs from the newer countries, to which they sent population, investments, capital and consumption goods. The importance of the industries of Western Europe gave that continent and the individual European countries an exceptional advantage. Industrial inventions came primarily from the United Kingdom, Germany and France. At the end of the century Western Europe was providing nine-tenths of the world's exports of manufactures. It has not, however, continued to do so. Before the Second World War the industrial output of Western Europe was one-third larger than that of the United States. In 1948 it was even less than three-quarters that of the United States. Over a longer period Western Europe's share in the manufacturing production of the world has fallen from 68 per cent in 1870, to 42 per cent in the period 1925–9, and to 35 per cent in 1958.

Important factors in the world economy before 1914 were the exchange of manufactured goods by the countries of Western Europe for raw materials and foodstuffs from the primary producing countries, and the willingness of those countries to develop their primary industries and to send their raw materials and foodstuffs to Western Europe. In many countries the dependence on foreign imports amounted to as much as one-fifth, one-quarter and one-third of their national income. If consideration is given to the countries of Western Europe as a whole, their dependence on foreign imports of foodstuffs is much smaller, but for certain key commodities Western Europe has depended greatly on imports from overseas. Between 80 and 90 per cent of textile materials, 30 per cent of timber, most of the non-ferrous ores and metals, nearly all the oil, and about 20 per cent of pre-war food supplies were imported from overseas. Approximately one-half of the United Kingdom's food requirements was imported, and of the world trade in meat 80 per cent went to Britain alone. Imports of some of the European countries expressed as a percentage of their national income in 1938 were as follows: Norway 32; Denmark 30; Benelux 29; Ireland 27; Greece 24; Switzerland 20; Sweden 18; France 13; Italy 10; Western Germany 10.

Dependence on foreign imports for its raw materials and foodstuffs did not make Western Europe vulnerable so long as she could rely on these supplies from countries which wanted manufactured goods, and so long as Western Europe was willing to provide in the exporting countries sufficient investments to meet the payments which the primary producing countries required to make to meet their import bill. This willingness to invest made it possible for the system of multilateral trade to work because Western Europe was able to buy from the Northern Hemisphere with dollars received from the sale of her manufactures in the other countries of the world, and the primary producing countries were able to buy manufactures in markets such as the United States even if the U.S. did not take their foodstuffs or raw materials.

So long as Britain and the countries of Western Europe maintained their industrial leadership, and their large hold on the world markets of manufactures which went with it, they had no serious economic problems. These problems began to emerge under a twofold pressure; the gradual industrialization of the countries of the world, particularly the primary producing countries; and the emergence of the United States as a power of enormous economic strength. It was natural that the thirty million people who emigrated from Europe to North and Latin America in the hundred years after the Battle of Waterloo would not always be content to grow foodstuffs and produce raw materials for industrial Europe. Moreover, investments, which were necessary for and resulted from the trade in manufactures of Western Europe, stimulated the growth of industrialization in the different countries of the world; and this industrialization was accentuated by the First World War, the economic crisis of 1929–31 and the Second World War. All of these changes in development affected the economy of Western Europe but the change was masked by the general expansion of trade which took place all over the world. World trade from 1913–39 increased as a whole, but the trade of each individual country did not necessarily increase nor did the trade in manufactures, food and raw materials increase to the same extent. For Europe the trade in manufactures is material. Between 1913 and 1939 the production of raw materials in the world increased approximately 50 per cent and the trade in them by approximately 25 per cent. During the same period the production of manufactures doubled, but world trade in manufactures did not increase and in the case seven of the chief manufacturing countries of the world, namely, Britain, United States, France, Sweden, Switzerland, Holland and Belgium, it fell by 20 per cent. In 1870 Europe had 13 per cent of the world's population, 68 per cent of the world's production of manufactures, and 90 per cent of the world's exports in manufactures. By 1938 Europe had 10 per cent of the world's population, but only 47 per cent of the world's production of manufactures and 55 per cent of the world's exports of manufactures.

Moreover, what trade in manufactures there was changed in character, which added another element of uncertainty. Prior to 1913 the exports from Western Europe entered directly into final consumption to an extent far greater than they did in 1958. Today there is a shift of emphasis towards exports of metals and engineering products so that a large proportion of exports from Western Europe are of capital goods. The trend in exports of consumption goods is towards goods of the luxury class. They can be sold in markets where there are large incomes and these markets are vulnerable to any economic recession. As these factors reduce the volume and the scope of the trade in manufactured goods, any realistic approach to the economic problems of Western Europe must acknowledge both the decline in the volume of exports from the countries of Western Europe to the other countries of the world, and the change in their character. As the world production of manufactures has risen, world trade in manufactures has formed an ever smaller proportion of the output. In the 1870's almost one-third entered into international trade; in 1913 one-fifth; in 1938 only one-tenth. Even by 1938 nearly one-half of the world's output of manufactures was produced outside Western Europe. Today, two-thirds of the world's output of manufactures is produced in countries outside Western Europe. Thus, by the end of the Second World War the decline of Western Europe in relation to the new world was real and complete. Only a major surgical operation could save the economies of the individual states.

(ii) Britain's External Position

In an article in the *Manchester Guardian* written in 1954 M. Bertrand de Jouvenel, while recognizing that the alteration in Britain's relationship with the outside world is partly responsible for her predicament, wrote: 'I can see nothing in the world situation that makes it impossible for

British skill and energy to earn the growing volume of imports necessary to a continuous increase of the national living standard.'[3] There is no truth in that assumption, and its uncritical acceptance by the British people and the British Government lies at the root of their failure to provide a solution to our many crises. The question raises a fundamental issue. Is it possible for British skill and energy to earn the growing volume of imports necessary to a continuous increase of the national standard, Britain remaining as an independent sovereign state? In the changed conditions of the world today, as the facts will clearly reveal, it is not possible for Britain as a separate independent state to sell abroad sufficient to be able to provide for her requirements of raw materials and foodstuffs, much less to provide for an increase in the national living standard. A growing volume of imports means an increase in the volume and/or value of our exports. That is difficult today, not because we cannot increase production, but because most countries which previously bought our exports (and this is particularly true of consumption goods) are not prepared to buy as many of them as previously, or if they do want to buy them they cannot pay for them without difficulty, or sometimes cannot pay for them in money tokens that we want.

As we have seen in the previous section, though world production of manufactured goods has more than doubled in the last thirty years, world trade in them has decreased. Over the last thirty years most importing countries have followed a policy of economic nationalism. They have organized their economy so as to be less dependent on supplies of manufactured goods from overseas. This applies primarily to consumption goods, but also to luxury and capital merchandise as well. This reflects itself in our commerce. In 1870 Great Britain had 2 per cent of the world's population, one-third of the world's production of manufactures, and two-fifths of the world's total exports of manufactures. By 1938 Britain had 2 per cent of the world's population but only one-tenth of the world's production of manufactures, and one-fifth of the world's exports of manufactures. And today we have a considerably smaller share of the world's production of manufactures and exports.

In the nineteenth century Britain was a very great world power, but the prosperity of her economy was dependent on an ever increasing world trade, particularly in manufactures. Today the two great powers of the world, the United States and the Soviet Union, are not to any considerable extent dependent for their well-being on external trade. This change in position and character has an important bearing on our chances of earning the money to pay for an ever growing volume of imports. British skill and energy were able to earn a growing volume of imports before the First World War. Imports were cheap. Britain was first in the field in the export of manufactured commodities and had few competitors. The newer countries wanted a wide variety of consumption goods as well as capital and luxury commodities; and Britain was always willing to finance the new countries in any of their purchases.

These features of world trade no longer apply. Britain is dependent for her prosperity upon the production and sale of manufactures in the world and on her being able to buy foodstuffs and raw materials cheaply. Since 1913 trade in manufactures has gone down by about 20 per cent. If we consider the post-war years the position is different but the result the same because of the fall in prices. Then the volume of world trade in manufactures rose by 33 per cent from 1953–7. It fell in 1958 but is now rising again, and so the 1959 volume is probably about a third above that of 1953. The volume of U.K. imports rose by 16 per cent, and of U.K. exports by 21 per cent, between 1953 and 1957. The value rose by 22 and 29 per cent respectively. In 1958 the value of imports fell by £29 million because of lower prices, the value of exports by £102 million. (Total imports £3,780 million, total exports and re-exports £3,355 million.) Thus the fall in prices put Britain in a very difficult position.

Looking at the matter in another way, the commodity imports and commodity exports in volume of both Europe and Great Britain were approximately the same in 1913. If, in the case of Great Britain, we take her imports and exports in 1913 as 100, then the average volume of imports into Great Britain in the five years before the Second World War becomes 125, but the average volume of exports from Great Britain for the same five years is only 65. And what is true of Great Britain is equally true of Western Europe. The volume of exports in relation to the volume of imports between these years was halved. In the five years before the Second World War the average inhabitant of Great Britain was importing 20 per cent more than he had in 1913, but was exporting 40 per cent less. Thus, as a result of the growth of industrialization throughout the world and in particular its development in the United States, the trade in manufactures throughout the world has been on the decline.

There can be no doubt that Britain is finding great difficulty in securing the cheap imports to which she was accustomed prior to the First World War, not only of foodstuffs but of raw materials as well; and hard put to it as she is to get cheap imports, she is unable to maintain her exports of manufactured goods in anything like the same quantity or volume. We do not export today (1959) as much as we did in 1913, and while there is a world market for capital goods and for quality goods to a limited extent, the market for the ordinary run of manufactured consumption goods, such as were by far the larger part of British exports in the past, cannot but remain a very narrow one. Britain has thus entered into a new period, one in which she cannot rely upon getting the same percentage of her national income from the sale of manufactures in the world, and in which she has to pay more for the raw materials and foodstuffs which she imports. It would be bad enough if only world trade in manufactures remained at its 1913 level. Britain's position is made more acute because not only has the amount of manufactures going into exports fallen, but the . price of imports has considerably risen, and it is to this question that we now turn.

(iii) The Illusion of Cheap Foodstuffs and Raw Materials

The most important factor which has changed the pattern of world trade since 1914 has been a change in the terms of trade, which have deteriorated considerably and which in 1951 became more unfavourable to Western Europe than at any other time. In 1946 the overseas terms of trade of Europe as a whole were in effect more favourable than in 1938. Since the war the terms of trade of all the member countries of the Organization for European Economic Co-operation combined together were as follows (1953 = 100):[4]

TABLE 1

| 1950: 95 | 1952: 97 | 1955: 100 | 1957: 100 |
| 1951: 92 | 1954: 100 | 1956: 100 | 1958: 105 |

In the case of the United Kingdom, the terms of trade improved by 25 per cent between 1913 and 1958 but, in 1958, they were 6 per cent worse than in 1938. But, as the United Nations report points out, movements in Europe's terms of trade do not, as yet, fully reflect the rise in the prices of foodstuffs and raw materials in relation to the prices of manufactured goods as expressed in price movements in the American market. This is largely due to the fact that the export prices of European countries have risen considerably more than corresponding United States prices while, in the particular case of the United Kingdom, foodstuffs and raw materials have been procured abroad at prices far more favourable than those ruling in the United States.[5]

Measured in terms of American price movements since 1938, the relative increase in the prices of Europe's imports compared with those of its exports would have been 27 per cent rather than 10 per cent in 1948, although the fall in American prices of primary goods would have reduced this deterioration to 22 per cent by the end of the year. Foodstuffs and raw materials could be purchased cheaply, but with the social development in the newer countries of fixed prices for bulk buying and an improvement in the condition of the agricultural workers, these favourable terms of trade no longer apply. It need not be represented that the unfavourable terms of trade which we in Western Europe have faced since the war will remain for all times. But the fact is that, although they may improve, Western Europe will never again enjoy the favourable terms they knew between the wars.

The population of the world, which has about doubled since 1900, is still increasing and between 1950 and 1957 it rose by 12 per cent. During the same period, the population of the O.E.E.C. member countries rose 6 per cent from 273·8 million in 1950 to 289·4 million in 1957. This increase means that the terms of trade will turn in favour of the primary producing countries and the policy of greater investment in primary producers' machinery will further adversely affect the terms of trade for the manufacturing countries. The primary producers are increasing costs of primary production themselves and so are affecting the terms of trade. The agricultural worker in Britain has had his wage raised from 30s. per week before the war to a minimum of 156s. per week and an average of 184s. per week in 1958. Naturally that rise over the years has affected the cost of foodstuffs in Britain. The farmer in the United States has guaranteed prices for his grain and foodstuffs. The steps taken in the United States and elsewhere to improve the wages and security of the farmer have been taken in every other primary producing country in the world. Thus, in the second half of the twentieth century we may expect that the cost of foodstuffs and some raw materials will be greater than it was in the first; that the favourable terms of trade which the manufacturing countries of Western Europe received, they will receive no longer; and that at the same time as the cost of their imports is going up, the countries of Western Europe will find that the prices for their exports are going down. Moreover, not only the terms of trade, but the content has altered also. With the development of industrialization the character of European trade has undergone a profound change. In the nineteenth century exports went directly into final consumption. This is not true today.

Mr. Colin Clark has dealt with the illusion of cheap food from the 1920's to the 1930's in very definite and specific terms in regard to Great Britain. But the illustrations which he gives with regard to Great Britain apply equally to the European countries and to the world as a whole. He measures the price of British imports in terms of the quantity of exports required to buy one unit of imports (terms of trade), taking 1913 = 100 as the base. This is quite a reasonable base, because the average for the whole period from 1900–13 was almost exactly equal to the 1913 figure. But it certainly does not represent a maximum. Earlier, about 1880, the terms of trade were much more adverse to Britain, and the figure stood at over 120. But for the 1920's the average came down to 80, and for the 1930's (likewise for the year 1938) down to 72. Unfortunately, as he points out, this state of affairs persisted long enough for people to come to regard it as normal. By 1947 the figure had risen to 84. The Marshall Plan was prepared in great detail in that year, based on the assumption, specifically stated, that the terms of trade would be good enough to remain stationary until 1952. By 1950 they had risen to 94, and by June 1951 to 111, i.e. rather more adverse than in 1913, but not yet as adverse as in 1880.[6] Although there has been some improvement since then, it seems out of the question that the terms of trade of the 1920's and the 1930's will return.

Professor D. H. Robertson has drawn specific attention to this problem when he comments on

how strong and persistent were the forces making it progressively more difficult for the manufacturing populations of Western Europe however correct their monetary arrangements, to earn from overseas the requisite fodder alike for their own fastidious stomachs and for their insatiable machines . . . we ought perhaps to have foreseen the emergence of the revolutionary notion that some day 1,000 million Asiatics would take it into their heads to expect to have enough to eat. But apart from these there seems to have been an almost unanimous conviction among Englishmen of every political party, and of almost every school of thought, that the days of cheap food would soon return.[7]

'Those who continue to believe that cheap food and raw materials are just around the corner,' concludes Mr. Colin Clark, 'are doing so in face of all the evidence, and must be held responsible for the consequences of any actions based upon this belief.'[8] There are people who would argue that the rise in prices which took place about nine years ago has been due to the Korean War, but this is a completely erroneous explanation. Before the Korean war broke out in June 1950 import prices for Great Britain and Europe were 70 per cent above the average prices of June 1946, and in the case of Great Britain devaluation only takes into account 15 per cent of the rise. Imports in the first quarter of 1951 were costing Great Britain at a rate of £800 million a year more than they could have cost at the 1946 terms of trade: a sum about equal to the whole of the defence expenditure of the country for 1950–1. The reasons for this were the world shortages of food and raw materials, which resulted themselves from the increase in world population. Some people argued that the world shortage of primary products was due to abnormal demands; but it would appear that the demand for primary products has not been growing as fast as it did previously.[9]

The following table shows the prices of certain commodities since 1913 and gives figures for ten of the main raw materials of the world for five years—1913, 1920, 1929, 1938 and 1958—and a look at these shows the extent to which the prices of these particular commodities have risen during that period:

TABLE 2[10]

Commodity	1913		1920		1929		1938		1958	
Copper (U.S. cents per lb.)	15·27	100	17·46	114	18·11	119	10·00	65	25·00	156
Cotton (pence per lb.)	7·01	100	23·14	330	10·26	146	4·93	70	34·00	500
Lead (U.S. cents per lb.)	4·37	100	7·96	182	6·83	156	4·74	108	9·00	206
Rice (s. d. per cwt.)	8/2	100	41/10	512	14/3	174	10/7	130	50/00	620
Rubber (s. d. per lb.)	3/0$\frac{1}{2}$	100	1/10$\frac{1}{2}$	62	10$\frac{1}{4}$	28	7$\frac{1}{32}$	20	1/11$\frac{1}{2}$	66
Tin (£ per ton)	201	100	302	150	207$\frac{7}{16}$	103	193$\frac{31}{32}$	97	735	365
Wheat (s. d. per qtr.)	31/9	100	80/7	254	42/2	133	28/11	91	72	—
Wood Pulp (£ per long ton)	15	100	51	340	17	113	12	80	45	295
Wool (pence per lb.)	9$\frac{1}{2}$	100	32	337	13$\frac{3}{32}$	138	8·9	94	89	950
Zinc (U.S. cents per lb.)	5·50	100	7·67	139	6·51	118	4·61	84	8·0	146

The best measure of the world demand for primary products is the index of world manufacturing production. In the forty years before the First World War, the production of manufactures grew at an average annual rate of 3·7 per cent, and world primary production grew at about the same rate. From 1913 to 1950 the annual rate of growth of world manufactures was 2·5 per cent. Today, world output of manufactures is currently about 40 per cent above 1950 having risen at an average compound rate of 4 per cent. The following table illustrates this trend:

TABLE 3[11]

Trends in World Trade, Population and Production since 1938

Volume Index 1953 = 100

Exports		1938	1948	1950	1951	1952	1954	1955	1956	1957
All commodities	...	70	70	85	95	94	105	114	124	131
Food and raw materials	...	93	79	95	98	93	103	111	121	127
Fuel	...	56	66	82	92	100	110	121	130	133
Manufactures	...	54	64	78	93	93	105	115	126	133
Population	...	82	93	96	97	98	101	103	104	106
Production										
Primary commodities		77	86	89	93	97	101	105	109	109
Manufactures	...	50	73	83	92	93	100	111	116	119

There is no way of escaping the conclusions to which the argument in this section leads. We cannot plan the economy of Great Britain over the next fifty years except on the assumption that she will need greater imports of raw materials and foodstuffs and that their cost will be higher. This fact, taken into account along with the position of world trade in manufactures, raises the whole issue as to whether a small country of fifty million people without any raw materials other than coal can, in the second half of the twentieth century, provide a decent standard of living for its people. Does the future lie with those countries of the world which, because of their large areas and large resources and large markets, are less dependent on world trade?

(vi) Large Areas and Large Markets

We have mentioned the decline of Europe and Britain in relation to the United States and the Soviet Union over the last fifty years. This, together with the increased nationalism and racialism, is the fundamental characteristics of the changes taking place in the world. What is the conclusion that the people of Britain should draw from the rise of these two giants? Britain is left at the present time as one of the states of Western Europe and not as a world power in the old sense. No amount of working long hours in Great Britain, even with a reduction in prices, is going to make the Australians or the New Zealanders or the Canadians buy manufactured goods from Britain, which they prefer to make themselves. The development of economic self-sufficiency and economic nationalism in the different countries of the world is making them try to provide themselves, as far as possible, with their own manufactures and those consumption goods which were our exports in the past. The two prosperous countries of the world are the United States and the Soviet Union. Let us, therefore, consider why they are prosperous, why they are virtually self-supporting, and why they are not confronted with the problems which beset Britain, in order to ascertain whether such a consideration throws any light on the solution of Britain's problems. It is not without point that the two largest countries of the world today are the two countries which are the least dependent on world trade. This was never true of Great Britain or of the world prior to 1914.

The United States and the Soviet Union have a number of characteristics in common. While the similarity must not be taken too far, as the United States is at present a much more highly developed country than the Soviet Union, nevertheless, the characteristics remain: a large area; a large population; great resources; and a highly developed and balanced economy. There are, of course, other countries in the world such as India and China which have the first three of these characteristics and may develop the fourth over the next fifty years, but at the present time the United States and the Soviet Union are the two outstanding countries of the world and they determine the nature of the twentieth-century world in which we live.

The first two characteristics, a large area and a large population, are apparent in both cases. It might be argued that the British Commonwealth has a large population and a great expanse of territory spread all over the world; but there is no real comparison between the Commonwealth as a political or economic community and the United States and the Soviet Union. The territories which Congress rules from Washington are in one continent, and the territories which the Kremlin rules from Moscow are all adjacent to one another and form part of one large federation. Large areas and large populations are obvious characteristics of the two great powers of the world, and in both cases we find one political authority governing the whole.

The third characteristic is that these countries are in the nature of being self-supporting and as such are able to produce the raw materials and foodstuffs which they require. To all intents and purposes the United States is a self-supporting country not dependent on world trade, and what is true of the United States is also true of the Soviet Union. In other words, the two powers whose foreign trade plays no noteworthy role in their economic prosperity, and whose foreign trade is in no sense vital to their economy, have become the only great world powers of the century.

An examination of the facts will soon demonstrate the truth of this proposition. There has been no period in history when the foreign trade of the United States has amounted to more than 10 per cent of its total production, and from examination of the figures of the past it seems fairly clear that the export trade of the United States will not represent more than 6 per cent of her total production over the next ten or twenty years. Thus, it is never likely to be of the same importance to the United States as it was, and in a sense still is, to the European industrial powers. The United Nations Economic Survey of Europe in 1958 provides a table which gives us the information shown in Table 4 on page 48.

What do these figures show? In the years immediately following the First World War, American exports represented not much less than 10 per cent of the total production. After the Second World War they rose substantially in absolute figures, but in spite of all the aid that the United States has given to Europe and Asia in the past few years, in spite of the large American export surplus, exports amounted in 1946 to only 4·9 per cent of the total U.S. product, and in 1947 rather more—namely 6·6 per cent—and in 1958 only 5·7 per cent, a percentage much smaller than in the years immediately after the First World War. The Marshall Plan and the Mutual Aid Programme have not brought about any fundamental change in this respect. Even in the first two years, when its costs were highest, when the U.S. financed the unusually large import surplus of Europe, U.S. exports did not even succeed in maintaining the 1947 level. Thus, although the Marshall Plan prevented any intensification of the European crisis which would have led to a considerable drop in U.S. exports and have endangered America's own prosperity, it did no more than that. The volume of U.S. exports as compared with the total U.S. product has not been fundamentally affected by the Marshall Plan.

Before the outbreak of the First World War Britain's total foreign

TABLE 4[12]

United States Production and Foreign Trade

(in billions of current dollars)

	After the First World War		Inter-War Period 1921– 1939. Annual		After the Second World War	
	1919	*1920*	*Average*	*1946*	*1947*	*1958*
U.S. Gross national product ...	81·6	94·7	84·3	203·7	228·2	450·0
U.S. total exports ...	7·9	8·2	3·6	10·0	15·1	25·6
Ratio of exports to gross national product (%) ...	9·7	8·7	4·3	4·9	6·6	5·7

capital investments were estimated to be around 3·5 billion pounds sterling, or between 17 and 18 billion dollars at the values then prevailing. The annual interest on foreign capital investment alone was greater than the total annual military expenditure before the First World War. Before the First World War Germany's total capital investments abroad amounted to about 30 billion marks at the values then prevailing. In 1913, at the pre-war peak point, Germany's military expenditure totalled about 2 billion marks—in other words, Germany's capital investments abroad were about fifteen times as great as her military expenditure, and the additional new capital investments made abroad each year were not much less than the total of military expenditure. In short, peacetime was the great period of European expansion.

The situation is very different today. After the Second World War foreign-political antagonisms are so acute that America's military expenditure even before the Korean War amounted to about $15 billion annually

—in other words, it was about as big in one year as the total sum of U.S. capital investments abroad. New private U.S. capital exports amounted to the following sums in millions of dollars: 300 in 1946; 700 in 1947; 1,000 in 1948; 400 in 1949; 621 in 1950; 528 in 1951; 850 in 1952; 721 in 1953; 664 in 1954; 779 in 1955; 1,859 in 1956; and 2,072 in 1957.[13] In other words, the military expenditure of the United States amounted to about seventeen times as much as private capital exports in any year taking the average of the twelve years.

Since the war we have seen an enormous increase in total Russian production:

TABLE 5[14]

U.S.S.R. National Income (i.e. material production)

1950 = 100

1951	...	112	1955	...	171
1952	...	125	1956	...	191
1953	...	136	1957	...	202
1954	...	152	1958	...	218

This may be due to a number of factors. Russia as a victorious power forced the defeated countries to pay her reparations in different ways; factories were dismantled and taken to Russia, both from Germany and Manchuria, and millions of prisoners of war were used for years both during and after the war to help rebuild Russia's devastated areas. Russia's army lived off the land in the territories it occupied, and in addition the countries in question had to pay reparations from current production without any consideration in return. Despite all this, the Russians have carried out the reconstruction of their devastated industrial areas without the aid of foreign capital, whereas considerable amounts of U.S. capital in the form of grants, loans and credits went to Europe. Lend-lease to the Soviet Union stopped as soon as the war was at an end, and with it the investment of any foreign capital in the Soviet Union. In spite of this, however, the rate of reconstruction in the Soviet Union did not lag behind that of the rest of Europe.

No other economic organization was as little dependent on the rest of the world as that of the Soviet Union. The very tenuous connection of the Soviet Union with the rest of the world through her foreign trade makes her reconstruction almost entirely independent of the great process of transformation that is going on outside her frontiers. Her five-year plans brought about a tremendous increase in industrial production, but at the same time the Soviet foreign trade was deliberately limited in volume, and does not assume a very large proportion of world trade (much less her own production) as the following table shows:

TABLE 6[15]

		1955 (million $)	1956 (million $)	1957 (million $)
U.S.S.R. Exports	...	3,469	3,669	4,381
U.S.S.R. Imports	...	3,061	3,613	3,930
World Exports	...	82,800	92,000	98,800
World Imports	...	88,200	97,200	106,400

The fourth characteristic which is common to these two countries is the growth of industrialization, mass production and standardization. No one suggests that you can compare what has been done in the Soviet Union with what has been done in the United States, but the principles applied remain the same. With a large market in both countries, great development has taken place in the increase of mechanization, standardization and mass production. The countries are self-sufficient for they can provide almost all their own foodstuffs and raw materials. In the case of foodstuffs they are large enough and their population is sufficiently numerous for them to develop any quantity of food production that the people require. Planning thus becomes a possibility. Anyone who follows the development of the Department of Agriculture in the United States will see the extent to which the state has promoted in many different ways the development of agricultural production, so as to provide the people of the United States with all the food that they require. In a similar way, though at a different level, the Soviet Union is doing the same thing, in spite of the fact that the standard of living in that country is very low, partly because it was low at the time of the revolution in 1917, and partly because of the enormous destruction that was wrought during the Second World War. But the low standard of living due to these factors does not affect the principle. Because of the large market, because of the large resources, because of the differences in temperature and climate, the administration in either the Soviet Union or the United States is in a position so to handle the production of foodstuffs as to satisfy the requirements of their own people. With the exception of France, perhaps, this is not true of any country of Western Europe; but it may, in the future, be true of India and China. And it could be true of a united Western Europe, particularly with the association of its overseas territories.

One of the lessons of the second industrial revolution is that a country which covers a large area and has a large population and a certain number of resources can create for itself a viable economy. Fifty years ago the

United States did not produce a lot of things which she does produce today. The two world wars of this century which cut her off from Western Europe made her produce many things which previously she used to buy from Western Europe. With a population of 174 million people occupying a territory larger than Western Europe there is practically no limit to the amount of foodstuffs which the American community can produce. The division of the world into primary producing countries and manufacturing countries which was a feature of the nineteenth century no longer applies today. The primary producing countries are no longer producing only primary products; they wish to be industrial as well. Therefore, the whole basis of the way in which the economy of the world developed in the nineteenth century no longer applies in the twentieth. If prosperity has come to the United States—as it has come—it is because certain fundamental conditions are found there. These are a large market, a free trade area within that large market, the removal of all barriers to trade between the fifty states, and a market operated by a common currency. If other areas of the world are to be equally prosperous—as they may be—the same conditions must be created. It thus becomes Britain's job to get into such an area in which those features are to be found or created. Some would say the Commonwealth provides such an area for Britain; others would say Western Europe provides such an area—that is the problem we have to consider now.

Britain is living in a changing world in which the great and prosperous are those with a large area and a large market, and who, while they are not self-supporting, are self-sufficient and in a position to control the economic potential which the variety of their resources and the numbers of their people provide. Britain has coal—plus some agriculture—as its only resources. How can she join a community like the United States or the Soviet Union? Is the Commonwealth or Western Europe the answer? To this question we now turn.

CHAPTER 3

Is Commonwealth Development the Answer?

'They are autonomous communities within the British Empire, equal in status, in no way subordinate one to another, though united by a common allegiance to the Crown, and freely associated as members of the British Commonwealth of Nations.'

Report of the Imperial Conference, 1926

'Our Commonwealth has a long history and some persons of a narrow political outlook assume—as they have done before—that it is approaching its close; but, if we take the true measure of human needs and dangers and opportunities in this age, we shall find ourselves summoned to make a new beginning.'

Sir Keith Hancock

'There is no doubt that mankind is once more on the move. The very foundations have been shaken and loosened, and things are again fluid. The tents have been struck, and the great caravan of humanity is once more on the march.'

General Smuts, 16th December 1918

'In what respects are our nineteenth-century outlook and our nineteenth-century techniques now obsolete? To sum up an infinity of detail under broad heads, we are living today in a period of revolution which has now been in progress for nearly two centuries and of which the two current phases may perhaps be labelled the social revolution and the colonial revolution.'

E. H. Carr

THE areas marked red on British maps have been in the past fifty years the British Empire, the British Commonwealth and the Commonwealth. Moreover, some of them have changed from being dependent territories to self-governing countries and positions of

52

independence. It is a unique world-wide community of democratic peoples from which the world can learn much. But is it wise to claim too much for it, as some people do? Has it taken on a form of permanent organization as one of the great powers of the world? Is the diversity of its peoples and climates something which makes it superior to the other great powers of the world? And will it provide a model in future for the political organization of the world? As it has changed so much over the last 200 years, to say nothing of the last fifty years, the questions which arise are: Will it remain static? Will it continue to change? Or will it break up altogether, and if so what will be the new beginning that it is summoned to make?

The Commonwealth is the product of the expansion of England which began in the early part of the seventeenth century. The first Queen Elizabeth had no overseas possessions. England lost her first empire, the American colonies, at the end of the eighteenth century. Her second, which developed from the emigration of British people from England, Scotland, Wales and Ireland to Canada, Australia, New Zealand and South Africa, today forms the British part of the Commonwealth. The colonial territories, in which non-British people predominate, were acquired over the centuries; many of them have obtained their independence, and others are in the course of obtaining theirs.

Until the First World War, the British Empire was a kind of partnership in which one partner, the United Kingdom, had 90 per cent of the assets and almost full control. As we have seen from Chapter 2 Britain was the principal manufacturing country in the world during the nineteenth century. She loaned money to any country that wanted it, and in consequence secured the lion's share of the trade of the world. British banks saw to it that people overseas were never short of money to buy British and European goods. The British fleet kept peace, where peace was kept, and the British mercantile marine in the main carried goods of all countries round the world. Although Britain possessed no raw materials except coal, she was strong enough in the economic sense to determine the peace of the world, and keep world order. But it was not a world government. It was a British government, and under the umbrella of this government England expanded and her colonies and empire and dominions developed.

The Commonwealth falls into four groups: first, the British Isles, which contains 51·7 million people in England, Scotland, Wales and Northern Ireland; second, the four so-called white dominions, Canada 16·6 millions, Australia 9·6 millions, New Zealand 2·2 millions, and South Africa 14·2 millions, of which the white population is approximately 2·9 millions; third, the dominions in Asia; India 392·4 millions, Pakistan 84·5 millions, Malaya 6·3 millions, and Ceylon 9·2 millions, and in Africa,

Ghana 4·8 millions, Nigeria 35·3 millions, South West Africa 0·5 millions, and Central African Federation 7·5 millions, which account for nearly one-fifth of the population of the world; and, finally, the dependent territories, about forty-three units of government for which the Colonial Office of the United Kingdom is responsible, and which amount to about 72·5 million people. These territories are dependent on the United Kingdom, and in no way are dependent on the other members of the Commonwealth.

Any proper review of the Commonwealth must examine these four groups, not only in relation to one another, but in the relationship to one another of the white dominions, the Asian dominions, and the territories which are dependent on and governed by Great Britain. For, despite the fact that it is a commonwealth of autonomous communities, it is the relationship of these communities to Great Britain that is important, for it is because of this relationship that the people in Britain look east and west to their associations and commitments all over the world.

It is considerations of this nature which make some British people genuinely oppose any effective political integration of Britain with the states of Western Europe, but, as we shall see, the relationship between Britain and the other states across the Channel in Western Europe cannot remain as it is at present and has been for many years. Some real and effective integration must take place. The dependent peoples are securing their freedom, and some, like Ceylon, may remain in the Commonwealth, while others, like Burma, will go outside it, and once this development is completed Britain's position will be substantially altered. The Asiatic dominions themselves will probably go their own way, so that we will see during the remaining decades of this century a great change in the relationship between the groups: the possible eclipse, perhaps, of Great Britain; the increased importance of India; the closer association of Canada, Australia and New Zealand with the United States; and the freeing of the dependent peoples from any kind of control by the mother country whether with or without any Commonwealth ties.

(i) Is the Commonwealth an Economic Unit?

We cannot understand the Commonwealth except in relation to its past, and particularly in relation to the way in which it has grown in an economic sense out of the development of Great Britain. The expansion of England meant the migration of people from the British Isles to those parts of the world which became the white dominions, the Asiatic dominions, and the present dependent territories. The greater part of the migration went to Canada, Australia, New Zealand and South Africa, but in the period between the two world wars this migration had ceased to be an important factor. Despite agitation for Empire development, it was soon found that Empire expansion was difficult after the First World War. As the newer Dominions were short of population the cry rang out for migration; but it was soon found that migration was of little value without money for the Dominions, and it was then found out that money was of little value without markets, again for the Dominions in the Commonwealth or in the world. Finally, as we shall see, people began to realize that the markets could not be confined to the frontiers of the Commonwealth, and the whole process of Empire expansion as such broke down. The frontiers had been pushed as far as they could be pushed, and while there was plenty of room for settlement in Canada and Australia, the economic conditions for this settlement just did not exist.

In the hundred years between the Battle of Waterloo and Gallipoli, of every three people who emigrated from Great Britain two went to the United States and one to the Colonial Countries or the Dominions—so that the British population of the overseas territories is greater in America than in the Dominions. Much is heard today about Empire migration, but in the ten years prior to 1939 more people came back to Britain from the Dominions than went away from Britain to them. The movement of population then was the other way, and there were reasons for it. Emigration is closely linked with trade, investment and economic policy. Recent tendencies in world trade, in Empire trade, and in industrialization, both inside and outside the Empire, have all had a limiting effect on the movement of population to the Dominions. If consideration is given to the investments of Great Britain it will be found that only 55 per cent of them (in terms of nominal capital value) are to be found within the Commonwealth and Empire, and only about one half of her trade; for, since Britain has investments outside the Commonwealth, such as in South America, it is essential for her to trade with them so as to receive a return on her investments. Thus, as 45 per cent of her investments are outside the Commonwealth, the trade of Great Britain must go outside the Commonwealth to a considerable extent.

There are other factors also. Britain is a large importer of food and raw materials, and a big exporter of manufactures. Since the Dominions cannot take the whole of the manufactured goods that Britain desires to export, she must find markets outside. These exports can be paid for only if the British people are prepared to buy goods from the countries to which the exports go. The trade between the Commonwealth as a unit and the outside world is not balanced, so there are very real reasons why Great Britain must trade outside the Commonwealth. Again, the Commonwealth produces more foodstuffs and raw materials than its member countries can consume. So the British Dominions export elsewhere, and become dependent to a certain extent on imports from other markets in the world. The dependence of Australia on the Japanese to buy wool, and the dependence of Canada and South Africa on the United States for manufactures, are two examples. In the economic sphere an Empire customs union is quite impracticable. The question is not one for Great Britain alone to consider. When the offer was made by Mr. Ernest Bevin, the Dominion Premiers lost no time in declaring that they were not prepared to have it at any price.

What will be the economic basis of the association of members of the Commonwealth in the next fifty years? The Commonwealth has vast resources and plays an important part in world production and trade, but it is not an economic unit. It produces more than it can consume. Today the Commonwealth produces 75 per cent of the world's tea, 50 per cent of its cocoa, rubber, wool and tin, 33 per cent of its copper and lead, and 25 per cent of its wheat, sugar and cotton, to mention some of its most important primary products. The countries of the Commonwealth provide 25 per cent of the world's exports, and take 30 per cent of the world's imports. But the Commonwealth as a whole cannot meet its own needs for some important primary products, e.g. cotton and tobacco; in the case of petroleum the Commonwealth is an importer but the sterling area so far has resources to cover all needs; nor can the factories in the United Kingdom and the other industrialized countries in the Commonwealth supply all the manufactures which its members require. Considerations of distance and transport costs often make it more economical for supplies to be obtained from non-Commonwealth countries. For certain specialized Commonwealth products markets inside the Commonwealth are insufficient. The trade of the Commonwealth countries with themselves and with the United States in 1957 can be seen from the following table:

TABLE 1[1]

		within Commonwealth		with U.S.A.	
		Imports	Exports	Imports	Exports
Canada	...	14	20	70	60
South Africa	...	47	52	20	7
Malaya	...	34	33	4	15
India	...	35	45	18	20
Australia	...	61	46	12	7
New Zealand	...	78	67	8	7

The belief that imperial preference (the system developed by the Ottawa Agreements of 1932) is an important bond between the countries of the Commonwealth, and that it does much to foster Intra-Commonwealth trade was widespread though today it is being more and more discredited. The fact is, indeed, that the increase in the trade of the Commonwealth countries since the Ottawa Agreements is more on the non-preference items. Moreover, the increase in Intra-Commonwealth trade after 1932 was not as great as the increase in world trade as a whole. The Ottawa Conference was the last attempt to preserve some kind of economic unity, but it has merely served to prove that the Commonwealth is not such a unity. The benefits and costs of imperial preference have fallen unevenly in the different territories and the whole system is now on the way out; some interests have calculated that since they have to sell a great part of their produce (e.g. Australian wool) in foreign markets, imperial preference has done them harm. The Ottawa Agreements provide no benefits to the British Commonwealth in general. They do not guarantee trade; they are not necessary for the development of Commonwealth countries. In short, the Commonwealth economically is not a unit, far less is it a self-sufficient unit.

The truth of this proposition can be seen from an examination of the change that has taken place in the exports and imports of the main areas of the world. World trade has continued to expand since the war, and the Commonwealth Economic Committee has produced bulletins dealing with Commonwealth trade over the years which give very interesting figures of the distribution of Commonwealth trade. If we treat Canada as part of the North American continent, and if we treat the United Kingdom as part of Western Europe for purposes of trade figures, Western Europe looms very large as a trading area and the rest of the Commonwealth becomes a very small trading entity indeed, and takes a very small part of world trade as a whole.

TABLE 2

Commonwealth and World Trade[2]

	Exports			Imports		
	1938	1949	1957	1938	1949	1957
World ...	100	100	100	100	100	100
U.S.A. and Canada	17·1	26·2	26·2	36·0	36·8	19·5
Europe and U.K. ...	47·4	40·1	40·5	56·1	47·3	43·2
Other British Commonwealth ...	11·3	11·9	12·3	11·6	14·6	12·9
Central and South America ...	8	11	8·7	7	1·0	8·7
Asia ...	10	7	7·5	10	0·8	9·1
All other areas ...	—	—	4·8	—	—	5·6

Canada, whose economic interests are now very closely tied with those of America, has an outlook much more North American than British. Canada, allied to the United States, has entered into a defence pact with the United States. Canada in 1921 passed an Act of Canadian Nationality to make Canadian nationality separate from and ahead of British. She aims to be an independent, sovereign state, and has refused to join in any federation of the British Commonwealth countries. The change that has taken place in the relationship of Canada to the United Kingdom can best be understood by a reference to the destination of the commodity exports and imports of Canada over the last few years, which shows an enormous change since the Second World War, but a much bigger change between the turn of the century and the First World War. An examination of the destination of Canada's commodity exports and the source of her commodity imports in recent years will show how great this change has been. For the five years before the Second World War, of Canada's exports one-third approximately went to the United States, one-third to Great Britain, and one-third to other countries of the world. Today 58 per cent go to the United States, 16 per cent to the United Kingdom, and 26 per cent to the rest of the world. In the five years before the war, of Canada's imports two-thirds came from the United States; today 69 per cent come from there, 10 per cent from the United Kingdom, and 21 per cent from all other countries.

It has often been pointed out that a prominent characteristic of the pre-war Canadian balance of payments on current account was its lack of balance by regions. While she was accustomed to run substantial surpluses with overseas countries, particularly the United Kingdom, she normally had deficits only slightly smaller in size with the United States. A consequence of the war was an intensification of this bilateral disequilibrium. Since that time, and due very largely to changes in the destination of her exports and the sources of her imports, the bilateral disequilibrium in her international accounts is still serious as the following table covering the last four years shows, and what is happening in Canada is only an indication of what will happen in the other three old dominions.

TABLE 3

Canada's current balance of international payments[3]
(million $)

		1955	1956	1957	1958
Total	...	− 698	− 1,366	− 1,400	− 1,112
of which:					
United States	...	− 1,041	− 1,640	− 1,551	− 1,204
United Kingdom	...	+ 341	+ 254	+ 142	+ 130

The following table shows the amount of investment by Great Britain and the United States in Canada, Australia, New Zealand and South Africa; and the change which has taken place over the last fifty years becomes abundantly clear.

TABLE 4

Estimates of current value of investments in Commonwealth countries given by local sources[5]

£ million

	From U.K.	From other countries (mainly U.S.)
Australia (1958) . . .	900	400
Canada (1957) . . .	1,064	5,177
India Pakistan } (1958) . .	400	700
South Africa (1958) . .	800	400

So long as the overseas territories of the Commonwealth were complementary to Great Britain the economic organization of the British Commonwealth worked. So long as the Dominions were prepared to grow the foodstuffs and raw materials which Great Britain and Western Europe wanted, and to take in return the products of their factories, the system could work. But it works no longer. It was a perfectly reasonable method of economic development in the eighteenth and nineteenth centuries, but with the passage of time the component parts of the Commonwealth, the Dominions, those others that are self-governing, and the dependent territories, have all desired to make themselves more self-sufficient, or to provide for themselves out of their own resources a greater part of their own manufactures. Between the two world wars we see the period which has been described by one critic as the great 'self-insufficiency of the Empire', and the attempt to put a barrier round the different countries of the Commonwealth, and make it a self-sufficient trading unit, has completely failed. Once the overseas territories ceased to be complementary new problems arose. At first it was thought they could be solved by the migration of peoples from Britain to those territories in order to make trade more complementary. But as explained above, it slowly dawned upon the politicians of the Commonwealth towards the end of the inter-war period that it was markets that mattered more even than men or money, and despite the large population of the British Commonwealth it has not a common market as has the United States or the Soviet Union. There are barriers round and between the countries of the Commonwealth, currency barriers, as well as barriers of export and import restrictions. All these barriers serve to underline the fact that the Commonwealth is not an economic unit.

In the days before the war we used to hear large claims by the Nazi leaders that they required colonies and the break-up of the British Empire. In a world of independent and competing national states, where colonial territories are of great importance to the prestige of individual states, the claim to colonies plays a part. If the greatness of a country depends upon the extent of its territory, or the size of the population it rules, or the raw materials of its colonial territories, then obviously any one country may, in such a competing world, gather within its control territories, coloured population, and raw materials. The expansion of Britain over the last 300 years set such a standard of national success for other countries to follow. Her expansion brought greatness, depending on a small number of white people ruling a large number of natives. If that is the standard of a country's success, how can one blame other European peoples and countries for following the example set by the first nation in the world— as it considers itself—if by following in its footsteps they can achieve the same kind of greatness?

Mr. Churchill said during the war that he did not 'intend to preside over the liquidation of the British Empire', but the question of the liquidation of the Empire must be faced squarely. The expansion of England, which began early in the seventeenth century before the union with Scotland, continued after the union as the expansion of Britain, and has been going on ever since. The British Empire grew to be one of the great powers in the world system based on capitalism, free enterprise, free trade, national sovereignty and sea power. That system reached its zenith in the nineteenth century, but now, at the end of thirty years of war, 1914–45, and fifteen years of the 'cold war', is on the verge of collapse. It belongs to the past and not to the future.

Moreover, the ideas which are moulding the future cause conflict within the British Empire. Since the Empire belongs to a political and economic age that has passed, why should it survive? It grew up under a certain set of world conditions. With the passing of those conditions, the question is, what form is it now going to take? The passing of empires is not new to the history of mankind. Britain began its expansion during the seventeenth century. It rose to its greatness or its maturity at the time of, and as a result of, the industrial revolution in which, of all the countries in Europe, Great Britain took the lead. It became the greatest world power at the end of the nineteenth century. Since the time of Elizabeth I, Europe has grown into twenty-six independent sovereign states. The world has grown into 123 states. The population of the world has grown in 1958 to 2,795 millions, of Western Europe to 277 millions, and of Eastern Europe to 95 millions. The economic and political structure of the world in which Britain enjoyed such expansion in the eighteenth and nineteenth centuries has come to an end in the twentieth.

(ii) Is the Commonwealth a Political Unit?

In his *Expansion of England* Seeley discusses the possible development of the British Empire. He speculates on what would happen if some of the British colonies were to separate from the mother country so that England was left on the same level as the states nearest to her on the Continent, populous, but less so than Germany and scarcely equal to France. Would it be possible for England to merge with the Colonies into a federal union? He writes:

In that case, England will take rank with Russia and the United States in the first rank of states, measured by population and area, and in a higher rank than the states of the Continent. We ought by no means to take for granted that this is desirable. Bigness is not necessarily greatness; if by remaining in the second rank of magnitude we can hold the first place morally and intellectually, let us sacrifice mere material magnitude.[6]

In the political sense the Dominions are each going their own way, and it is a mistake to suppose that we can create an exclusive organization standing alone. A federation of Great Britain and the Dominions, which was what Seeley had in mind, has never been acceptable to the Dominions, even if it would be acceptable to Great Britain. Mr. Joseph Chamberlain was an Imperial Federationist, so were others in his time. The Australian

Premier, Mr. Deakin, tried unsuccessfully in 1908 to interest the Commonwealth in a common government. Australia and New Zealand have each refused to modify their sovereignty by creating a federation of the British Commonwealth. Early in 1944 Lord Halifax, when Ambassador to the United States, made suggestions in a speech in Canada that a common policy should be framed and executed by all governments of the Commonwealth in 'foreign policy, economic affairs, colonial questions and communications'. These items are, of course, fundamental to sovereignty and comprise the chief power exercised by the governments of Great Britain and the Dominions.

Mr. Mackenzie King, replying, made it quite clear that it was not acceptable to the Canadians:

> I maintain that apart from all questions as to how the common policy is to be reached and enforced, such a conception runs counter to the establishment of effective world security and therefore is opposed to the true interests of the Commonwealth itself. We are certainly determined to see the closest collaboration continued between Canada, the United Kingdom and the other Commonwealth countries. Nothing that I am saying should be construed as supporting any other view than this. Collaboration inside the British Commonwealth has and will continue to have a special degree of intimacy. When, however, it comes to dealing with the great issues which determine peace or war, prosperity or depression, it must not, in aim or method, be exclusive in meeting the world issues of security, employment and social standards. We must join not only with Commonwealth countries, but with all like-minded states if our purposes and ideals are to prevail. Our commitments on these great issues must be part of a general scheme, whether they be on a world basis or regional in nature. We look forward, therefore, to close collaboration in the interests of peace not only inside the British Commonwealth but also with the small friendly nations outside it as well as the great.[7]

Australia and New Zealand have entered into a pact with one another for their own defence of a kind which they have not been willing to enter into with Canada and Great Britain, which suggests that the peoples of Canada, Australia, New Zealand and South Africa are not prepared to modify their political independence as did the Welsh, the Scots and the English centuries ago. A conference took place in London between the representatives of the Dominions and of Great Britain on the question of defence in May 1946, and Mr. Lionel Curtis, a strong believer in the Commonwealth and Empire, maintained that they had demonstrated at least one or two points:

> They have shown that the traditional system of Commonwealth security has completely and finally broken down. At this critical time, when the question hangs in the balance whether a third and even more calamitous war can be

prevented in the next generation, no real Imperial Conference could be held. The United Kingdom no longer commands sufficient resources to discharge the pledge it gave to their predecessors at the last Imperial Conference in 1926. How many people today are aware of that pledge? I should say that not one per cent of citizens in the five sovereign states of the Commonwealth know that in 1926 all their governments signed a report saying: 'In the sphere of defence the major share of responsibility rests now, and must for some time continue to rest, with His Majesty's Government in Great Britain.' Since their first publication these words have scarcely ever been mentioned in Parliaments or in the Press until last Thursday, when *The Times* quoted them in a leader. Dr. Evatt, the Australian Minister for External Affairs, analysed the report in his broadcast of May 10th, but he omitted all reference to these crucial words, which govern the whole report.[8]

Defence is the most vital question on which it might be thought the Commonwealth countries would come together, but here there is little chance of unanimity or of an agreed policy, even between the white dominions and Great Britain, and even less between the white dominions, including Great Britain, and the Asiatic dominions. Canada has always been more anxious to associate in her defence effort with the United States, and created a joint board with the United States before any such authority had been created with Great Britain; and A.N.Z.U.S., the Australian and New Zealand and United States Defence Pact, to which Great Britain is not a party, is the factor on which the defence of the two Pacific dominions relies.

Before the war the defence of the Commonwealth was carried on by Great Britain and paid for by the British taxpayer. Since the war we have been lulled into a certain state of illusion by statements issued from time to time after meetings of the Commonwealth Prime Ministers, when a Commonwealth defence policy was being discussed. But that policy has now been finally buried. Lip-service may still be paid to the principle of strong Commonwealth co-operation in all aspects of defence, but that is about as far as it goes. It was thought, particularly in Great Britain and particularly among the Conservative Party, that the Suez Canal was a great Commonwealth artery which in the hour of danger would be defended by aid rushed to it from all parts of the British family of nations. We now know how futile that conception was and the ruin which followed the attempt to put even a small part of it into operation. Even if Canada, Australia and New Zealand were not looking to the United States for their real protection in the second half of the twentieth century, they have little to offer in the way of defence, for the figures still show that the weight of the Commonwealth defence burden is borne by Great Britain. It is difficult sometimes to get up-to-date figures about the forces of any country, but it would seem that the strengths of the forces are as follows:

TABLE 5[9]

(Figures in 1,000)

		Navy	Army	Air Force	
U.K.	...	101·5	303·9	173·4	(1959)
Canada	...	19·9	47·2	51·7	(1958)
Australia	...	10·8	20·9	14·8	(1958)
New Zealand	...	3·0	4·4	4·8	(1958)
Pakistan	...	7·2	125·0	(small)	(1956)

Up-to-date figures for the other member countries are not available

It is considerations of this kind that make one realize that the partnership is breaking up because the senior partner can no longer carry the burdens which she carried in the past, and because the other partners are either unwilling to carry them or to be fully associated with one another in any kind of union. Among the Asian dominions, India and Ceylon desire to follow a policy of neutrality, and to avoid any entanglements with the West or with North America at all. The Pacific dominions, with Canada, are associating themselves more and more with the United States. South Africa is too unstable a factor to be taken into any account in any question of the defence of the Commonwealth as a whole, because of the uncertain position which exists in that country. Her future lies with Africa, and that means with black and not white Africa. Eire remained neutral during the war, and has now left the Commonwealth, as has Burma. We are, therefore, left witnessing the gradual break-up of a family of nations, which is an inevitable stage in the course of its development. If the individual parts of the Commonwealth had been prepared to sacrifice their sovereignty and create some kind of federal government for the Commonwealth as a whole, this break-up would not now be taking place. The fact that they were not prepared to do so shows that the different areas and territories want to and will get their own separate and independent ways.

Thus the British Commonwealth is not a super-state with a legislature and executive authority. Rather it is a political community in several senses, and the sovereign status of its members does not alter the truth. The great problem is that of defence. The Second World War showed that the Commonwealth cannot defend itself. It survived and won the war only with the help of the United States and the Soviet Union. With the exception of Canada, because she has the United States next door, it is extremely doubtful if any one country of the Commonwealth can defend itself. Australia today, with a population of 9·6 million, inclines towards the United States, as do New Zealand and Canada. And for the next fifty years those three countries will come more and more into that orbit, and move from Great Britain's orbit. And what does the future hold for South Africa as a continuing member of the Commonwealth?

Canadians, Indians, Australians, United Kingdom subjects, have to register as such for passport and other purposes. If the Commonwealth is to be a political organization in the world, one would expect to be looking towards a common government for matters of common concern, but the members are moving further away from that conception. Recent suggestions for a political union, even of the loosest kind, have been turned down by Commonwealth members. Would the United Kingdom be sufficiently interested in any of the parts of the Commonwealth to give up some of its sovereignty in order to form a Commonwealth government so as to have one Commonwealth authority, if only in the field of defence? The answer to this question is a firm 'no', but we do well to ask ourselves that question when thinking about Britain's relationship to Europe at the present time.

On many major questions in the world today it is impossible for Commonwealth Premiers to come to a general agreement, much less one that is enthusiastically unanimous. Britain's attitude, or that of the Australian Government, is different from that of the Government of India on the question of recognition of the Chinese People's Government. The Australians will not allow the Indians to settle in their country. When South Africa absorbs a certain part of African territory against the wishes of all the other Commonwealth countries, and flouts a decision of the High Court of the United Nations and then refuses to abide by decisions of the United Nations, what action does 'the Commonwealth' take? Is Britain, or any of the Dominions, prepared to enforce a decision of the United Nations against India about Kashmir, or against any other Dominion? The states of the American Union had a civil war to preserve the Union. Is the Commonwealth such a political organization that any member of it will ever go to war to preserve it?

(iii) The Colonial Peoples

In the Commonwealth we are faced not only with the self-governing Dominions and those emerging into self-government, but with those countries who still remain under the Colonial Office and who have not yet achieved either self-government or independence. Moreover, we know that the wide differences between those countries and Britain or the white dominions lie not only in that they are dependent but in that they are very, very poor. If the income per head per annum in Europe is $680, then in

Africa it is barely $70, and in South East Asia barely $60. Poverty and dependence are the characteristics of these colonial peoples.

The per capita daily intake of all foods in calories is shown for the following countries (India, although independent, may be taken as typifying the standards of living of the colonial territories):[10]

U.S.A. (1957)	...	3,100
U.K. (1957/8)	...	3,290
India (1954/6)	...	1,890

The per capita consumptions of textiles (wool and cotton), based on industrial consumption of the raw materials in the following countries were for 1957-8:[11]

U.S.A.	...	24·0 lb
U.K.	...	22·9 lb
India	...	5·3 lb

How can feudal societies be converted into high-standard-of-living countries and democratic communities at the same time? This is the problem which confronts the Western countries all over the world—a problem whose solution is essential for the harmonious development of our time. In the normal order of things, the development of backward peoples would inevitably result in the termination of any status of subservience. How is it to be done? The dependent territories of the European countries are scattered throughout the world, and they became the responsibility of the great powers at various times since the seventeenth century with the expansion of Europe. Most of them were secured during the latter part of the nineteenth century. The central purpose of British policy is to guide their colonial territories to responsible self-government within or outside the Commonwealth, in conditions that ensure to the people a fair standard of living and freedom from oppression. If this is the purpose of the other countries of Western Europe, then there is no problem except one of time. In due course self-government will be realized in all the colonial territories of the European countries.

Certain territories of the European countries are looked at in a different way because they have strategic value. During the expansion of England it was important to control the Mediterranean area because of the interests in India, and the need for using the Mediterranean and the Suez Canal. So Great Britain acquired Gibraltar, Malta and Cyprus. A kind of control was maintained over the Suez Canal just as the United States controls the Panama Canal, and the Soviet Union wants to control the Dardanelles, but British control of Suez is now a thing of the past. When Britain carried trade to Asia, apart from acquiring India she acquired Singapore and

Hong Kong. Subsequently, she found that to hold Singapore she must also have control of Malaya, though she did not understand that before the Second World War, and did not properly prepare for its defence. If Britain is asked why she held on to these territories, the reply will be that if she had not done so others would. The United States claims Formosa as an essential strategic territory in her Pacific defence. The Russians claim the Kurile Islands for the same reason. How long can individual countries, in view of the world-wide colonial revolution that is taking place, hold on to strategic places of this kind?

The day is past when one group of people belonging to the West can use their power, position, money and resources to control territory which rightly belongs to others, or to take wealth from peoples in parts of the world who, owing to their ignorance and inability, are unable to profit from it. In the eighteenth century, in the early days of colonial development in North America, and later in Australia and Canada, the greater share of the benefits which came from the economic development redounded to the people of Great Britain, or in Europe, as the case may be. This has been a large part of the story of colonial development in the past, but it is a story which will not be repeated in the second half of the twentieth century.

The yearly output of copper in Northern Rhodesia in 1937, all of which was sold outside Northern Rhodesia, was worth about £12,000,000.[12] Of this £5,000,000 went in dividends to shareholders who were all non-residents; £5,000,000 was paid in royalties to the British South Africa Company, which happens to own all the minerals in the colony by virtue of a treaty made forty years ago. The benefit of the industry from the point of view of African consuming power is to be found only in what was paid in miners' wages, and by that part of European salaries spent on hiring domestic servants, which amounted to £350,000 in all. Even when all the indirect benefits to Africans are taken into account, their gross gain can hardly be put higher than £1,000,000. This procedure in the case of copper is typical of the pattern of behaviour of the West in overseas dependent territories whenever mineral production is concerned. The Western powers appropriate the natural resources. They develop them in their own way and for their own purposes and benefits, and their ways generally ignore the pre-existing structure and function of the society where the development takes place. Of the wealth produced the Western European carried out of the country about £11 for every £1 he left behind. Call it trusteeship, call it development, call it imperialism or anything you like, but the fact remains that it is not going to continue in the second half of this century. While it may be true that the West has brought some benefit to the peoples of India, Africa and Arabia by its association with them in the field of development, yet it is equally true that the dependent territories suffered both as importers and exporters from the exploitation of the West.

The political changes of this century mean that this type of rule must end. So long as Britain and the other European countries controlled the government of the overseas territories of the world, such as South East Asia, Africa and the Middle East, the benefits from this relationship accrued to the Western powers. But now if money is provided for development programmes, it will be spent for the benefit of the peoples in the countries themselves. If it leads to increased food supplies, it will not mean an increase necessarily for Europe, but for the peoples of the territories first, and these territories will begin to export their surpluses only after their own needs have been satisfied. This is a complete change in the economic relationships of the different countries of the world and of the peoples of the world and it will have both a profound effect on the lives of the people in China, in India, in Africa, in Arabia, and South East Asia, and also a profound consequential effect on the standard of living of the peoples of the West.

The colonial revolution which has been taking place in the last fifty years has become a revolt against political, economic and racial inequality. Colour is at least as important a factor as political freedom or economic equality, for the colonial revolution to which we refer is a revolution of people who are coloured. Those territories of the world which were occupied by European peoples—Canada, Australia, New Zealand—in the course of their development, have all acquired self-government. The countries to whom this was denied in the early part of this century were the countries with a native population which had been brought under the influence of one or another of the European powers. Thus, the first step in the colonial revolution has been of a political nature. Demands for the withdrawal of the capitulations in Egypt and Turkey; demands for self-government in India; demands for the abolition of the unequal treaties in China; and these political demands have not been abated. Everywhere today where European nations still exercise any kind of political rule over backward peoples, the demands for political independence are more and more insistently raised.

The right to self-government was expressed in a very notable speech which the Foreign Minister of Pakistan, Sir Mohammed Zafrullah Khan, made at the United Nations meeting in Paris on the 16th November 1951, in which he said, 'Go to the help of your brother whether oppressor or oppressed.' When asked in what manner may the oppressor be helped, he replied:

Restrain him from proceeding with oppression. In the instance we have in mind the 'oppressor' is not an individual or a nation: it is a false notion, a vicious principle, an immoral relationship, which today is universally condemned and repudiated, but which in actual fact obstinately persists in fouling the channels of human intercourse and in breeding ills and disorders, which continue to frustrate and discount all beneficent effort towards the promotion of human welfare. It has been designated by various names. We prefer to describe it as domination and exploitation of a group by a group, a people by a people, a race by a race, in any sphere of human relations, political, economic, religious or other. Its most familiar instance is colonialism or imperialism. We approach this problem from a purely human point of view. In our judgement any relationship, whether established by the use of force—direct or indirect—or the employment, let us say, of diplomacy—not to use any harsher description—even though evident by the articles of constitution, convention, treaty, engagement or agreement, if it has resulted from domination or exploitation, is vicious and evil and must be speedily terminated. Such a relationship operates to degrade both the dominator and the dominated, the exploiter and the exploited. No arrangement can in our view claim moral validity which is not arrived at between the representatives of free people occupying a position of equality vis-à-vis their opposite numbers and subject to no pressure or coercion of any description. . . .[13]

'Had the people of England,' said Mr. Gladstone, 'obeyed, and proceeded to eschew violence and maintained order, the liberties of this country would never have been obtained.'[14] No one will argue that Mr. Gladstone was a Communist, and yet he was pointing out that in the process of the development of the freedoms of the British people, violence had played its part. He could have quoted at the same time Mr. Jefferson, the author of the Declaration of Independence, and one of the early Presidents of the United States, for in many letters he dealt with the question of rebellion and the need for rebellion in order to bring about change: 'A Little rebellion, now and then is a good thing, and as Necessary in the political world as storms in the physical. . . . It is a medicine necessary for the sound health of government.' 'What country can preserve its liberties, if its rulers are not warned from time to time, that this people preserve the spirit of resistance? Let them take arms. . . . The tree of liberty must be refreshed from time to time, with the blood of patriots and tyrants.' 'The late rebellion in Massachusetts has given more alarm than I think it should have done. Calculate that one rebellion in thirteen States in the course of eleven years, is but one for each State in a century and a half. No country should be so long without one.'[15]

Mr. Justice Douglas in *Strange Lands and Friendly Peoples*, written after his tour of Arabia and India, points out that Asia is in revolution, that there are rumblings in every village from the Mediterranean to the Pacific:

A force is gathering for a mighty effort. We think of that force as communistic. Communists exploit the situation, stirring every discontent and making the pot boil. The revolutions which are brewing are not, however, Communist in origin nor will they be even if Soviet Russia is crushed through war. *The revolutionaries are hungry men who have been exploited from time out of mind. This is the century of their awakening and mobilization.* What I saw and heard as I travelled this vast territory that lies under the southern rim of Russia reminded me very much of what I had read about other revolutions. The spirit that motivates these people is pretty much the same spirit that inspired the French and American revolutions. The abuses against which our American forbears protested in 1776 were piled high. They are listed in our Declaration of Independence: dissolution of legislative bodies by the King; corruption of judges; maintenance of a standing army and quartering of troops among the people; imposition of taxes without the consent of the colonies; transporting citizens beyond the seas for trial of offences committed here. These and other practices of the King brought our people to a boiling point; and we declared ourselves free.[16]

This, of course, is the position: the complaints of the people in Africa, in Arabia, or in South East Asia, though different from those of the Americans in 1787, are just as important, and the list is very long. The absence of medical care; the absence of schools; land reform; the desire to learn how to farm the modern way; the right to vote; the right to elect a representative government; the power to expel and punish corrupt officials. All these, and many more, reforms are involved in the nationalism which is spreading all over these different territories, and which serve as a challenge to us all which we must accept.

The desire for self-government will be realized in all parts of the world where it does not now exist over the next fifty years. When the American colonies broke away from Great Britain they united in a federation which has grown into the greatest power in the world. If the federal idea had been conceived in the thirteenth century, Europe might have gone through the centuries under one common government, developing its ideas of democracy, united, instead of divided into twenty or thirty independent separate states. Some of the territorial boundaries in such regions of the world as Africa, Arabia and South East Asia cannot be justified on economic, social or political grounds. They are geographical boundaries created by the occupying country at the time of the occupation, and they will, if maintained, prevent the development of self-government being treated in each of these regions as one problem, as it should be, and not as a number of separate problems for each territory, as it is being treated at the present time.

Thus we may conclude that in the not too distant future the Western powers—and chief among them Great Britain—will see their colonial peoples achieving both self-government and independence; and with that independence a federation, perhaps, of a large part of Africa, of the Arab world, and in South East Asia. There will be a reduction in the number of places coloured red on the map, and new communities will arise out of the liquidation of what has been the British Commonwealth and Empire.

(iv) The Future of the Commonwealth

The Commonwealth of Nations has been a great and successful political experiment, and is as fine a demonstration of the way in which self-government for dependencies can be made a reality as anyone could wish to see. But it does not follow that the form which the British family of nations developed is necessarily that which the world could adopt. For in what way can we apply the circumstances of Great Britain and her eight dominions to the circumstances of the twenty-five states of Europe, let alone to independent states of the world? We cannot apply the British principle to the continent of Europe. Great Britain has permitted her dependencies to grow up, to have self-government, and to work together by the mechanism of the Imperial Conference. That experiment has worked, but that is not to say that we can apply the same principle to Europe, and for example allow Germany, or any other state, to be the senior partner in any organization for the purpose of solving the problems of Europe.

Sir Keith Hancock spent eight years surveying British Commonwealth affairs. To the question whether the British Commonwealth offers any pattern for the world, he replies:

> The sanguine orators of 1919 announced that their Commonwealth possessed the secret of international association in peace and freedom. They had offered their Commonwealth as a model to the world. But the statesmen of 1936 knew that the world had not the least intention of copying the model. . . In short, the experience accumulated between 1919 and 1936 exposed the optimistic illusions which had been prevalent at the end of the war. It would be too much to say that the facts of 1936 were a refutation of the Commonwealth theory of the imperial partnership. But they did refute the universalization of this theory, the translation of it into a model of world government.[17]

We get ideas from the British Commonwealth, but not the form of world government. At the same time one of the most interesting experiments in the government of states and in international co-operation is the British Commonwealth of Nations.

'The British Empire,' General Smuts said, 'is the only successful experiment in international government that has ever been made. . . . It is a congeries of nations . . . not merely a state but a system of states.' Many suggest that the method adopted by the members of the British

Commonwealth provides a solution for the problems of national sovereignty, and that the principles of government by consultation between nations, as worked out in the British Commonwealth, should be applied to the other nations. It has developed a loose organization which combines the government of the parts in such a way as not to restrict freedom and liberty of action of the individual states of the Commonwealth. Yet can we adopt the methods of consultation used by the members of the British Commonwealth of Nations to develop a European Commonwealth of Nations in which France, Germany and the other powers would be members? The answer to this question is, unfortunately, no. If the idea of the British Commonwealth of Nations had been acceptable to the nations of Europe, the League of Nations would have succeeded. For the League gave the European nations the opportunity to settle their differences by consultations of the same kind as those which take place between the different members of the British Commonwealth. The differences which exist between the states of Europe are much greater and more fundamental than those between the older members of the British Commonwealth.

The British Commonwealth of Nations has developed out of the British Empire, which in turn has grown from Great Britain. The people who populated Canada, New Zealand and Australia were mostly English-speaking people. The Commonwealth began with the settlement of the colonists under the British Crown, and under the British Parliament. Thanks to the common sense and liberal instincts of the British Parliament, the separate Dominions have achieved the status of self-government. But the Crown still remains the common factor in the system of government for the Empire as a whole. Thus the members of the British Commonwealth offer no parallel to the other states of the world. There is no group of nations in the world which could link themselves together as the states of the British Commonwealth have done. The Commonwealth works by consultation, with the senior partner in real control. The League of Nations provided adequate machinery for consultation and co-operation, by which the nations could have developed a political organization along similar lines. But the European nations did not take advantage of this opportunity; the elements making for conflict were stronger than those making for co-operation. In the success of the British Commonwealth, the dominant position of Great Britain has played a large part. With the exception of the United States, which is outside Europe, there is no other state to play a similar role. Nor, if there were, would it be permitted to play such a part in the development of a European Commonwealth.

With the presence of the world conditions under which it expanded and grew, Britain was at first independent of Europe. Today she is no longer. Once she could defend herself unaided; today she can no longer.

Once she was the greatest single unit in world trade; today she is no longer. Furthermore, the supremacy Britain wielded in India,. Africa and Asia can no more be maintained. India and several other countries have their independence and the remaining colonial peoples seek theirs. What future is there for the old Empire in this new world? What new form will that Empire assume? It must be clear, therefore, that since the turn of the century the great period of the expansion of Britain is over. If the world is to remain a community of independent sovereign states, competing with one another for power, then—while Britain may have been on the winning side in World War I and World War II—she cannot go on winning one world war after another. Both world wars have demonstrated her dependence on other powers, more so the second than the first.

Moreover, the British Commonwealth of Nations provides in fact no real form of political organization in the twentieth-century world. Many refer to it loosely as a 'federation', which, of course, it is not. A partnership, in which the power and the capital reside in the senior partner, it may be; but no world power can exist as a kind of partnership in which one of the major members has the power, the authority, the wealth and the strength, as Britain in the Commonwealth has even today. For Britain is a part of Europe. As such she must play her role in the political and economic organization of Europe. So long as she was able, during the last 300 years, to preserve the balance of power in Europe, so long was it possible for her to avoid competing with, or taking part in, any political organization on that continent. But war is the sanction of the balance of power, and it is doubtful whether Europe can continue to be a battlefield in view of the developments of modern warfare. If civilization could survive twenty years of continuous warfare at the end of the eighteenth and the beginning of the nineteenth centuries, it could not do so at the end of this century. For, with atomic bombs, nuclear weapons, the new means of delivery, and all the other paraphernalia of modern war, European civilization will be unable to survive a repetition of two such world wars as the first half of the twentieth century has already witnessed.

If, therefore, the balance of power as a system of political organization has outlived its usefulness, something must be substituted in its place. Europe must look either to a federation or to some form of association which will be able to provide a proper political and economic structure for the Continent as a whole. Britain—not the British Commonwealth, but Britain—must play her part here, not only for her own benefit and full development, but for her survival, for without her co-operation there is no satisfactory solution to the many political and economic problems in Europe of which she forms a part.

Finally, following the revolution in Russia and the development of Communism in the Soviet Union and China, and with the spread of the idea of freedom throughout the world, colonial territories can no longer be viewed as a permanent feature of our political system. The peoples in the colonial territories are no longer satisfied now to be dependent on the older empires. With the general development of the political freedom of the colonial peoples, including those in India, 90 per cent of the British Empire strikes out on its own and seeks to be independent of Whitehall. And with such developments taking place the British Empire, both as a geographical expression and as a political entity, comes to an end.

Nevertheless, while the Commonwealth is in process of dissolution, it need not necessarily disintegrate. The ideas which it developed over the last four centuries are a major contribution to the political development of the world, but the spread and further development of these ideas does not depend on the continuance of a British Commonwealth or Empire. Clearly the British Commonwealth is not a menace to the peace of the world. It is not directly endangering the lives of other people, out of hunger for more territory, or ambition for more power. It does not have a warlike nature in the sense that other nations have shown themselves to be warlike in the last fifty years. But it does stand in the way of world order. So long as the Commonwealth maintains its present political form there can be no peace in Europe because Britain will not play her part constructively in the building of European government. So long as the Commonwealth remains as at present constituted, there will be a struggle within it in Asia and in Africa, which, both in the political sense and the economic sense, must inevitably promote conflict in other parts of the world. It no longer, as it did in the nineteenth century, provides a form of world order or has a fleet sufficient to preserve it. Moreover, Britain, the centre of the Commonwealth, can no longer preserve her own solvency or provide a viable economy for her own people as she did heretofore.

In the quotation at the beginning of this chapter Sir Keith Hancock, taking a long view of the Commonwealth, points out that if we take the true measure of human needs and dangers and opportunities in this age we shall find ourselves summoned to make a new beginning. That is the great opportunity which both Great Britain and the Commonwealth have at the present time, but, since the Second World War, there have been few signs that they are prepared to seize the great opportunity open to them. A new beginning does not necessarily imply that the Commonwealth should proceed as a country amongst other countries like the United States or the Soviet Union. We have already argued in the two preceding sections of this chapter that it is not an economic unit, and that there is no ground for thinking that it will develop any kind of political organization which would make it a federation similar to that of the United States or the Soviet Union. What, then, shall be the form which the new beginning takes? It is very necessary to face realities in regard to this question, as the illusion of the Commonwealth is perhaps one of the greatest illusions from which most British people suffer.

The realities which we must face are not very many in number. The migration which made the expansion of England over the centuries has now stopped in the sense in which it operated in the centuries gone by. True it is that Australia and Canada will look for migrants over the next fifty years, but the greater part of the increase in their population will come from their own residents, and in any event the migrants will be of an assisted character quite different from the migration which took place in the nineteenth century.

When we look at the strategic problems of the world, the Commonwealth divides itself very dangerously into two very specific blocks—the white members of the Commonwealth, and the new Asian and African members. Australia and New Zealand, for example, though far distant from Europe, look at the problem of association with the United States and the general defence against Russia, China and Communism in a way which is little different from that of Britain. Some of the Asian dominions are opposed to N.A.T.O. and regard it with distrust as an alliance with imperialist America. The proposals for a Pacific N.A.T.O. have not been welcomed by India, though they have been welcomed by the white dominions in the Pacific. No one who has travelled in the Asian dominions can fail to be conscious of the universal distrust of America amongst the Asians, particularly in India and Pakistan, and whilst Pakistan has agreed to take military aid from the United States this only serves to increase the distrust which the Indians feel. She is regarded as the imperialist successor to Great Britain, and as such she suffers from all the distrust that Britain suffered from in the past.

But the differences between these two groups in the Commonwealth are made even greater by post-war events. Between 1945 and 1950 Britain was almost moved to associate with the states of Western Europe on account of the events in Eastern Europe, particularly the seizure of Czechoslovakia. Thus, to Great Britain, Russia is the real enemy for, so far, however wrongly, China is not greatly feared. The Chinese entry into the Korean War was excused in Britain as self-defence against America. The most notable aggressive war today is in Algeria conducted by the French as a colonial war. This naturally throws together the representatives of the Asian dominions, and leads them into severe conflict and differences with the representatives of the white dominions. For, as the years go by, we will learn more and more that the differences in outlook between the Asian and the other members of the Commonwealth are very difficult, if not impossible, to resolve.

There is a further factor which must as time goes on have its effect on the ultimate unity of the Commonwealth. If there is one thing which holds the Commonwealth together it is that different countries have developed their Commonwealth unity in a belief in parliamentary democracy and equality. It is the factor of democratic equality which is the chief unifying force in the Commonwealth today, apart from the Crown. Thus, unless the Commonwealth is to stand for equality in all its aspects, this basis will be attacked. It is, however, difficult to see how it can be maintained. The problem of race relations is of the first importance. What is happening in South Africa, in other parts of Africa such as Kenya, and the Federation of Rhodesia and Nyasaland, and the colour bar which exists in different member countries, including Great Britain, naturally influences the attitude which the Asian members adopt towards the other members of the Commonwealth. While they agree that some separation of races is tolerable, for after all Hindus and Moslems are separated into the distinct states of India and Pakistan, and while they admit that backward peoples cannot be given immediate equality, nevertheless none of the Asian dominions is prepared to accept the idea that there could be any permanent or prolonged subjection of any of the native peoples of the world by European powers. That, as one critic has expressed it, was 'totalitarianism' of the Commonwealth ideal. It is difficult, therefore, to see how so diverse a group of peoples can maintain even the front of unity in the face of world events during the next fifty years. The very size and potentiality of India puts her in the position of a great power, probably greater than any other member country of the Commonwealth. With India an independent republic and the dependent territories granted their freedom, we are only left with the white dominions and their association with Great Britain, and where will this development lead?

If we are to develop towards some kind of world government on a regional basis then obviously the Commonwealth cuts across these regions. Sir Keith Hancock has pointed out in his development of the Commonwealth how the problems of nationalism and sovereignty, which are the two problems which confront the countries of the world today, have prevented the Commonwealth from coming together in some kind of political organization. If the Commonwealth could survive in that form, then obviously it would provide a form of political structure which the rest of the world would join, or which would absorb the other nations of the world. The fact that it has not been able to do this only goes to show that it does not provide the solution which is required in the way of a world political organization. It is foolish to build it up into something which it is not. If the United Nations cannot succeed because the nations refuse to surrender their sovereignty, then a loose organization like the Commonwealth does not provide any alternative solution.

If we are to be realistic, we should examine the four groups of the Commonwealth and see what sort of new beginning they can make.

A common sovereignty to the Crown; the development of common political institutions based on real political freedom; and the establishment of self-government in areas where it has never been established before, are all contributions of a major character to the political development of the world. If we look at the four groups of the Commonwealth we can see the new beginning and the contribution which it could make to world development in the second half of the twentieth century. We have already examined the declining position of Great Britain, and have argued that it should join some kind of European union. South Africa will ultimately become part of an African political organization, and with it will go most of the dependent territories which are situated on that continent. If these two developments were to take place, if Britain were to join a political union of Europe, and if some kind of political authority were created in Africa for Africa as a whole, little remains of the Commonwealth apart from the Asian dominions with their independent outlook on the one hand and Canada, Australia and New Zealand on the other hand, which, as we have already seen, are becoming more and more linked to the United States.

The Commonwealth has a chance to make a new beginning today, but it will make it in individual sections, each playing its own part in building some kind of political organization in its own part of the world; but the individual countries can bring to the regions where they are the political experience and wisdom which they have acquired over the centuries as a result of the development of democratic institutions which came from the expansion of Britain.

CHAPTER 4

A New Science of Politics

*'A new science of politics is indispensable to a new world.
This, however, is what we think of least; launched in the
middle of a rapid stream, we obstinately fix our eyes on the
ruins which may still be descried upon the shores we have
left, while the current sweeps us along, and drives us
backwards towards the gulf.'*

Alexis de Tocqueville, 'Democracy in America'

I N THE previous chapters we have examined the decline of Europe
in the twentieth century and the problems which confront Britain,
now no longer a great power, in her struggle for survival in a world
which has seen so many changes unfavourable to Britain over the last
fifty years. We have argued that survival in the future depends largely
on the merger of countries in the same area, so that countries will be
created with large populations and resources, such as are to be found in
the United States, the Soviet Union, China and India. Finally, in search of
some such development for Britain, we have considered the nature of the
Commonwealth to see if, by closer association, it would provide the
necessary political development, which is at present lacking, only to
conclude that the Commonwealth provides no real answer and that some
other solution must be found. In this chapter it is proposed to examine the
nature of several supra-national political authorities; for if we are to
decide Britain's future political development in relation to the other
countries of the world, we must examine the principles on which any such
policy should be determined.

Modern democracy dates from the Middle Ages, for with the establishment throughout Europe of Christianity it was assumed—though it may
not have been realized—firstly, that all human beings had an equal right
to derive benefit from the social system, secondly that all adults had an
equal responsibility for its maintenance, and thirdly that there was a
certain unity in Western Europe itself. These three ideas form the basis
of any democratic society, though it does not follow that all three of them

78

are to be found anywhere in the world in any one area, or that any one of them is to be found in every part of the world.

The responsibility for the maintenance of society and the right and duty which each person has in respect of that responsibility is, of course, the political aspect of democracy. Freedom in the political sense is the product of Western civilization. It developed in Europe and spread over the different parts of the world, partly to the North American continent and elsewhere by European migration, and partly by the growth of what was first the British Empire and later the British Commonwealth. When movements of people take place, ideas move with them; but over the centuries these ideas may develop in the new or adopted countries differently from the way they develop in the older countries from which they came. Thus the people in the new world have ideas and characters and ways of life which are very different from those of the people in the countries from which their forefathers came. One of the principal ideas which has developed out of Western civilization is that a society which boasts of political freedom must provide for its people the conditions in which that political freedom can live and grow. Such a society must consist of people who believe in setting other people free. For, in the free world, man is more than a citizen of the state, and the state must be recognized for what it is, namely one aspect, and not the most important aspect, of the individual's life. As democracy is a form of government in which political freedom is a very important element we must ask ourselves when we talk of the democratic world or the free world to what extent political freedom is characteristic of the different areas of the world. What political freedom as we understand the term in Western Europe and North America is to be found in the Soviet Union, Eastern Europe, Latin America, India, China, South East Asia, Africa and the Middle East? A close examination of the political institutions in those regions will show many different concepts, of which some at least appear quite irreconcilable with those of the West.

The equal right to derive benefit from the social system is the economic aspect of democracy. The right, of course, was quite clear in the Middle Ages and the economic system then protected it to a certain extent. It was lost with the Industrial Revolution, but with the spread of political democracy it is being recognized more and more today. The welfare state, however, which has developed in some form or other in some of the states of Western Europe, in the Soviet Union, in the United States and in some of the countries of the Commonwealth is the response of people to this idea. Thus, though we may not have found any satisfactory way yet by which people can derive equal benefit from the fruits of the economic system, attempts to secure that equal benefit are being made in various ways in most of the different continents of the world.

While many people acknowledge the political and economic attributes of democracy only a few realize the importance of the principle of unity both in providing political stability and giving an opportunity for its economic development. In the early days the experiences of the Christian Churches suggested the unity of the world and the need for an all-embracing society if its benefits were to be fully obtained. While these ideas developed among the peoples of Western Europe they were not applied there. It was left to the peoples in the American colonies to demonstrate what unity amongst a number of states (at first thirteen and finally fifty) and a common government could mean for the political and economic development of a democratic community. For, with all the faults of the American federal constitution, as Lord Acton has pointed out, the development of the principle of federalism has produced a community more powerful, more prosperous, more intelligent and more free than any other which the world has seen. Had the states of Western Europe at the end of the eighteenth century united in a federal union as did the colonies across the Atlantic, how different would have been the history of the world in the nineteenth and twentieth centuries?

While political freedom and social justice are necessary elements in any democratic society, they are not enough. If a society is to be stable, it is essential that it inhabits an area adequately blessed with raw materials and economic resources, and that it is composed of a population large enough to provide a market which will service the material needs of the community. This is the third attribute of democracy, and a society which is to be properly described as democratic must be able to satisfy these conditions; for, in the modern world, political freedom and economic justice, necessary though they may be, are not enough; they only take us two-thirds of the way. The community which calls itself democratic in the twentieth century must be large enough in population and in area to secure stability without which the political institutions and economic conditions would, in themselves, be of little value. Whether the governments of the United States and the Soviet Union provide for their people political freedom and social justice we need not consider at this stage. At least those two powers by their federal systems provide that third attribute of a democracy which was a feature of Western Christendom when the foundations of modern democracy were laid, namely unity over a large area.

(i) The United Nations Fallacy

We have had in this century two attempts to create some kind of world organization. Both attempts were products of the two world wars and

both failed; for, to prevent world wars we must have international governments, and that requires both the proper machinery and the will to work
it. So far we have had neither. The United Nations is composed of too
many countries varying in size and in living standard and power; and it is
based on the sovereign equality of those individual states as if sovereignty
and equality were fundamental to the composition of a world organization. Furthermore, an organization based on the sovereign equality of
the separate states as they exist in the world today brings together peoples
who are completely unlike one another and who cannot make the same
contribution to the organization to which they belong. If there is to be
freedom and equality between nations, each one should be independent
of the others and equal in strength, size and power.

Economically the United States is as strong as the rest of the world
put together. As we have seen, the conflict which pervades the present
world is a conflict between the capitalist society of the United States and
the so-called free world on the one hand, and the Communist society of the
totalitarian Soviet Union and its satellites on the other. In so far as these
countries are members of the United Nations it must be obvious that they
use such power and strength as they have to absorb other countries into
their sphere of influence. The Latin American countries side with the
United States. The satellites and some of the Asiatic countries side with the
Soviet Union. Thus, no problem is really solved; and the matters which
come before the United Nations Assembly are discussed not by a parliamentary body, as they should be, but from the point of view of the
balance of power and the interest of the individual country concerned, and
the group to which it belongs.

National sovereignty is the problem which any political advance in the
world must attack and tame. Any regional or world political authority
to be effective must have power to deal with those political and economic
questions which the member states cannot resolve by themselves, because
they affect their relations with other member countries. Insistence on
state sovereignty is a much greater cause of evil in the modern world than
capitalism, Communism or Fascism. National sovereignty is the condition-
ing cause of the renewed preparation for war in the world today and of the
fears, suspicions and hatreds which follow the preparation for war. Nor
does the presence of the umbrella of the United Nations in any way
interfere with the truth of this proposition; for the preparation for war
and the fears, suspicions and hatreds which follow the preparation for
war are greater in 1959, after fourteen years of the United Nations, than
they were in 1945, and what is true today of the United Nations was
equally true of the League of Nations in 1939.

An association of states is no substitute for government. It does not
contain within its machinery even the germs of government. Government,

as we understand it in the democratic world, means an assembly elected by the people and responsible to them, which has power to take decisions which it can make effective. An association of states, big and small, which have no common factor in their political thought, drawn from all parts of the world from peoples of different race, religion and state development, is incapable of converting itself into a body of this kind.

The United Nations is ineffective also because it is without power to carry out its decisions. The essence of government is that, once a decision is made, force can be used in order to see that the decision is carried into effect. Without the policeman there would be no law and order; and if there is to be any kind of world authority it must have a policeman, which means it must control the defence forces of the world. This does not mean it must control the police forces of Chicago, or of Milan, or of Stalingrad. It means that it must have sufficient power, i.e. aeroplanes, tanks, warships and military personnel, to be able to maintain law and order between the different regions of the world should any of them come into conflict. There is a fundamental difference between an authority which has its own armed forces and an authority which has to ask for volunteers from its members to secure them. The nations of the world are not prepared to give to the United Nations the control of their armed forces. Until they are willing to do so, the United Nations cannot be an effective body for keeping the peace.

It may be argued that the Security Council could have created in the United Nations a sufficient defence force for its purposes. Anyone who argues that way must be either blind to the reality of the present position between the great powers, or unwilling to acknowledge the developments which have taken place. The United Nations was based on the conception of great-power unity. It was thought that the Soviet Union, the United States, Great Britain, France and China would agree, and so the veto was inserted in the procedure of the Security Council. As the great powers have been unable to agree, the use of the veto by the Soviet Union has meant that the Security Council could not function as an executive body. Thus an attempt was made to transfer its business to the Assembly; but here again its success has not been very encouraging. While the United States was able to arrange for a United Nations police force in Korea, it was able to do so only by providing 95 per cent of the force itself, and the resistance to North Korean, Russian and Chinese aggression in Korea has been more a military operation of the United States than an exhibition of collective security by the members of the United Nations. For the Soviet Union is not willing to pool its armed forces with the other forces of the world, nor is the United States willing either. The United Nations has never been anything other than an association of states; it has never had any real or effective power; it is not and never will be a government in the sense that the Federal Government of the United States or the Politbureau of the Soviet Union can be regarded as a government.

Finally, the United Nations is ineffective as any kind of world organization because it cannot provide adequately for the economic and social changes which must inevitably take place in various parts of the world. An association of eighty countries, with their boundaries defined, some prosperous, some independent, some dependent upon the others, presupposes a static world community and does not take into account the changes which over a period of years must come about. The United Nations, as at present constituted, is incapable of dealing with the changes which must inevitably take place over the next fifty years. It cannot give freedom to colonial peoples, or provide for the proper political development of Africa or the other backward territories of the world. In other words, any international authority which is to be effective must have the competence, the authority and the power to be able to deal with economic and social problems as they arise and to resolve them. And that an association of states can never do.

(ii) *Is World Federation Premature?*

Many people who will agree with the criticisms of the previous section and find the United Nations inadequate to meet the needs of our age will argue that world government should be secured by the application of the federal principle, and that if the Charter of the United Nations were altered so as to provide for a world federation, the machinery thus created would be capable of resolving the international conflicts with which we are faced. The proposition so stated, however, begs the question; for while a world federation could provide adequate machinery for this purpose, we must consider whether, in a world which is divided between Communists, non-Communists and neutrals, such a solution is politically feasible, and if it is why it was not embodied in the Charter in 1946.

Federalism is a method of dividing powers of government so that the central and regional governments are within a limited sphere co-ordinate but independent. The test of the principle is: does it embody the division of powers between central and regional authorities, each being independent of the other? The principle is seen applied at its best in the United States of America, Australia, Canada and India. It is doubtful whether it applies in the Soviet Union or in China, as their regional governments are in the last resort not independent of the central government. Once we are clear as to what the federal principle means, we must then ask what are the appropriate conditions in which the principle can be applied, and once we know what the conditions are we must ask the further question as to whether these conditions are world-wide and are to be found in every country or continent in the world. There are three main conditions which must be satisfied if the federal principle is to be applied successfully, and when these have been examined we shall be in a position to answer the second question as to whether they are to be found in each of the countries of the world.

The first condition is, of course, that there is a desire among the people who are to be parties to the federation to bring certain aspects of government under common control. A federation is not a league or an alliance or an association of nations. It is quite a different thing from the British Commonwealth, or the Council of Europe, the North Atlantic Treaty Organization, or the United Nations. Peoples and states come together in a federal system of government where they have certain matters which they desire to be dealt with, not by the individual states themselves, but by one authority for the whole of the peoples and the whole of the states. The desire springs from a number of problems— military security is one. The idea of common defence appealed to the American states at the end of the eighteenth century. Associated with this is, of course, the desire to be independent of foreign powers, and that independence may only be realized where a number of states come together in a union instead of remaining separate. As was said in the formation of the American Constitution: 'Unless we hang together we will hang separately.' Apart, therefore, from political matters there are economic advantages which can be obtained by a number of states and a number of peoples coming together and forming a common market. Here again, the United States is a very good example.

When we come to examine the factors which create a desire for union, we shall find a number of factors quite absent. Community of language, of race, of nationality, and of religion, are not necessary factors to be present when people come together in a federal union. The United States of America was not a nation in 1788 by any modern standards, nor was Canada, or Switzerland. In fact the differences of language and of race, of nationality and religion, are among the factors making for the adoption of the federal system, and what applies in these matters applies equally in social standards and social institutions. It is not necessary for these to be similar in each of the federating states, because in the main social standards and institutions are matters reserved for the regional authority.

When we look at the world, obviously the desire for union is applicable to the world as a whole, as there are a number of matters which today, if they are to be dealt with effectively, can only be dealt with under one common control. The emergence of the atom and the hydrogen bombs has made the need for a world authority in military matters essential if law and order is to be preserved and a third world war is not to break out. The economic crises which perpetually confront different countries and continents in the world show how necessary it is for us to get some kind of common control in matters of money and tariffs, and the development of a freely functioning world market. Here again the experience of the United States in the last 150 years shows the benefits that can accrue in the economic field from bringing together economic matters of this kind. If, therefore, the desire for union in certain major political questions is one of the conditions which must be satisfied if a federal system is to be applied, then we can answer in the affirmative so far as the world is concerned. It may be the world is not ready for it, but these are matters which could better be dealt with under common control.

In a federal as opposed to a unitary system of government there must be a number of factors which make it desirable, if not necessary, for certain sections of the federation to demand that they retain their full sovereignty over certain matters. Where there is no community of language, race, nationality and religion, obviously this demand arises. A Government of Canada could never have been obtained with the French Catholics in the east and the English Protestants in the west, unless the provincial governments had been retained, and these matters left to the provinces and not brought under the control of the central authority. There are, of course, a number of other factors which make people who desire to come together in one form of government for certain matters desire to retain their independence in others. Where many of them have previously existed as colonies, or as independent states, they desire to keep their independence.

In other cases where there is a divergency of economic outlook, primary producing states and manufacturing states, while prepared to merge their identity in certain matters, still want to keep some of the political questions under their own control, and geography is a factor too, as in the United States and Australia, where areas are too large for the people of the borders to be governed by a parliament thousands of miles away. It follows from this that the divergencies that exist between people go to make the success of a federal system.

When we come to apply this generally to the world it will be quite clear that these divergencies exist, and the desire to retain power over a very large number of political questions would always be present if the federal system were applied to the world as a whole. If we could contemplate a world federation, the federal authority having powers in matters of armaments and trade, but nothing else, the divergencies between the areas of the world are so great that they would want to retain most of their legislative power in their own hands, as it would be impossible to get a common government on a unitary basis for people who are as different in their ideas as the people of the U.S.S.R. and the people of North America.

This brings us to the most important condition which has to be satisfied if a federation is to be successful. In the first place there must be some similarity in the social and political institutions and some agreement as to the basis of their form of government. The American states were all republics, the Australian states were all part of a constitutional monarchy, and so they were able to come together. Moreover, they were all democratic both in a political and an economic sense. Thus they did all have in the main a capacity to work together, but this capacity to work together cannot survive extreme divergencies, and the United States provides the best example of this. At the time of the union two things were left open: slavery, which was left as a matter for each state to decide itself, and whether a state could break from the union of its own accord, and these matters were never properly clarified. As Lincoln pointed out at the time of the Civil War: 'A house divided against itself cannot stand. This government cannot endure half slave and half free, it will become all one thing or all the other.'

Similarity in political ideas is, of course, essential to the working of any federal system, and, when we come to apply that principle to the world, we find it does not exist. The peoples of Western Europe and North America are democratic in the sense that they have maintained the principle of freedom as the basis of their system of government; they have assumed that all adults are equally responsible for the maintenance of government, and they have assumed in the main that all human beings have an equal right to derive benefit from the social system of the community. Thus, just as the United States could not be half slave and half free, so no federal world could be half democratic and half totalitarian as it is today. Until there is the highest common factor of agreement on political thought between the peoples of China and the peoples of the Soviet Union and the peoples of North America and the peoples of Europe, no federal system of government could be contemplated, because democracy means one thing to the Communists and another thing to the peoples of the West.

In the second place, when we look at the capacity of people to unite, the size of the areas and their economic resources is not unimportant. It would be foolish to suggest that a federation of the world made up of some eighty-eight states could be organized today, where some of the units are very large, with great populations and great resources, and other units are very small. The reference in the Charter of the United Nations to the sovereign equality of all peace-loving states must, as Professor Carr has pointed out, be regarded as evidence either of a high degree of political simplicity, or as a scarcely less discouraging readiness to pander to popular superstition. Albania is not the sovereign equal of the United States, nor of Brazil, nor of the Soviet Union, and this example could be multiplied many times. Like the right to freedom, the right to equality applies to individuals and not to nations. Nevertheless, the areas of some of the states that make up the world are so small as to be unsuitable for the application of federation to the world as a whole, but it may be that by the development of regional areas we can contemplate a series of regions over the world, which, if they were democratic, could come together in a gradually developing pattern of world federation.

A sense of community has been developed in depth over a wide area to support institutions of government in India, China, the Soviet Union and the United States, but the last country is by far the best example. For without the institution of the federal government the United States would not have developed as it has. Cannot a similar federal institution be created in Western Europe, and perhaps in other areas such as Latin America, Africa and the Middle East? A federation of Western Europe, of which Great Britain was a part, would create one government over a wide area of 280 million people, among whom a sense of community already exists.

The Security Council does not satisfactorily represent the peoples or governments of the world. Red China is not a member, and France and Britain, who are members with a veto, certainly do not speak for Europe. If the Security Council were to consist of representatives from North America, India, China, the Soviet Union, Western Europe, Eastern Europe, Latin America, Africa, the Middle East and South East Asia, it could provide an institution capable of arriving at decisions binding on, and supported by, the peoples of the world. Moreover, with the creation of these regional institutions, war would be banished within the individual regions, and there would be a possibility that the world-wide institution created on the basis of the regional organizations could in the long run prevent war.

If we wish to expand the United Nations community, there are at least two problems to face: first, it should embrace all the peoples of the world regardless of colour, race, religion or ideology; second, it should consist of institutions through which the views of the individual peoples can be made effective. If the United Nations were founded on the federal institutions of ten such great areas of the world, we would resolve both these problems. Such governments would provide law and order in their own regions, which, covering large populations, would have a sense of community, and we would begin to see the creation of institutions which had a basis in reality, and which were capable of resolving the economic and national problems out of which wars arise. With this development it would not be impossible to make the Assembly of the United Nations an elected body—elected by the people in each region—which is impossible today because of the great disparity in size, resources and stability of those who are members, and because of the absence of those who are not. Thus, an effective world organization being premature, we can work towards it by creating regional organizations which have a sense of community and which function over a wide enough area to make them both effective and stable.

Finally, it is important that any unit in a federation should have sufficient resources to make it viable; it is not enough that a state should be part of a federation with rights given to it by its constitution, it must have sufficient resources to be able to maintain the rights given to it. It is this factor which has been overlooked by political scientists in discussing the federal system, but it was made quite clear a long time ago by Alexis de Tocqueville. He wrote:

> The chief circumstance which has favoured the establishment and the main-tenance of a democratic system in the United States is the nature of the territory which the Americans inhabit. Their ancestors gave them the love of equality and of freedom, but God himself gave them the means of remaining equal and free by placing them upon a boundless continent.

What de Tocqueville meant was that the boundless continent had enabled the Americans to fulfil the promise of mobility. Democracy made this promise, but the riches of America fulfilled it, and a democratic system, like any other system which can survive only when its ideals are realized, survived in America because an economic surplus was available to pay the democracy's promissory notes. These conditions are not to be found in many countries of the world. They are not to be found in any one of the individual states of Western Europe, including Great Britain; but a federation of Western Europe, including Great Britain, would bring together the economic resources and a large common market which would make Western Europe economically viable as none of its individual states is today.

We are therefore faced with the dilemma that while there are a number of matters of common concern which would make the federal principle applicable, and where there is sufficient divergence equally to make it applicable, the conditions are not present in the world, either politically or economically, which give the states of the world the capacity to federate. An advance must be made along two lines. In the first place, the states of the world must be organized in larger regional areas. If Latin America, Western Europe, Africa, Arabia and South East Asia come together in some form of federal government, then the world would be organized in twelve or fourteen groups of states which would be economically viable, and which from the economic point of view could be states in a federation because of their need for a common government and their need to remain separate. But here the second principle applies, and that is that there would have to be by each of these regional governments and areas an acceptance of the democratic way of life, and an acceptance of the fundamental principles of human rights and freedom, which are the legacy of the West. There can be no political combination between peoples who believe in democracy and peoples who believe in totalitarianism, or peoples who believe in freedom as against tyranny. Democracy has three attributes: politically, the right of freedom and of self-government; economically, the right of each human being to derive equal benefit from the social system; and the federal principle as well, but the federal principle can only be applied to the world when the states and peoples in it have accepted the other two.

We are left with Western Europe as an area in which such a regional federation might be created. World federation being premature, let us work towards the union of democratic countries which occupy the same area in order to increase and improve the political organization of the world. Some such unions exist, be they democratic or totalitarian. Can Western Europe develop that way too as one of the democratic federations?

(iii) Matters of Common Concern

The size of the unit of government, in the past, has been dictated largely by geographical conditions. People who lived together as a community organized themselves politically as a community. Europe was at first divided into a large number of units, and then gradually their number was reduced. At the end of the eighteenth century Germany consisted of some 118 states. In Italy there were about half as many, and previously France had been similarly divided. By the end of the nineteenth century Italy and Germany were united and Europe consisted of about twenty-five independent states. The size of the unit of government should be determined apart from geographical considerations by the functions which the government has to exercise. It should be determined by the nature of the work to be done, not by conditions of its geographical or historical inheritance. As civilization develops communications become more important and easier; roads and transport over a large area are brought under the control of one common government; and thus the areas needing common governmental control have, over the last few centuries, become steadily larger.

At the present time the success of a common government dealing with matters of common concern, such as defence, currency and customs and the like, in the United States and in the Soviet Union, is a lesson to the other countries of the world. We have a world in which in North America, in effect, there is one government; in India and China and the Soviet Union there are governments covering very large areas and a great number of people. But in Western Europe, the continent from which most of the civilization of the world had its beginnings, there are divisions of a political nature which the history of the last fifty years has shown to be holding back the development of the Continent as a whole. And what is true of Western Europe is true of Africa, South America, South East Asia and the Arab states. The insistence on independence and sovereignty of small peoples, in small areas, with small and powerless governments, leads to instability. So the extension of the area of government may become an essential element in democracy. Local governments to look after local affairs; national governments dealing with those matters that extend beyond the boundaries of local authorities; regional governments looking after such matters as customs, currency and defence; possibly a world government which would provide, for example, for a world police force, world currency and the freeing of trade barriers all over the world.

'The gravest issues confronting us, therefore,' writes Professor Tawney, 'if complex in detail, are in principle simple. The first is to reconcile the ecumenical liberalism, which is a property, not of any group or party, but of the history of Western Europe, and whose fruits are civil liberty, tolerance, and political democracy, with the tasks imposed by the emergence of a mass technology and the obligations of the welfare state.'

The second is:

To win general recognition for the truth that departments of life which, in a not distant past, could reasonably be regarded as the exclusive province of a score of separate governments, have been converted by the changes of the last two generations into matters which, to be handled with effect, must be treated as affairs of common concern. It is to do on a grand scale for a Europe cabined and confined in a maze of restrictive nationalism what was done, on a narrower stage, when economies crippled by the obsolete fetters of provincial particularisms, municipal liberties, and seigneurial franchises were submitted to the unifying control of authorities with wider horizons and a more inclusive grasp. An integration of Europe, whatever its precise form, which broadened the basis of her economy, eliminated customs barriers and competing currencies, and enabled the basic industries of food, fuel, iron and steel, and engineering to be organized to serve a market of two hundred million persons, would unquestionably be followed by a general increase in economic prosperity and political strength; but the particular sacrifices and temporary embarrassments entailed by it would not be a trifle. Reason is on its side: but the natural human egotisms of interest and emotion; of locality, class and occupation; of regional loyalties and national pride, will rally to resist it.[1]

Anyone who reads or listens to the debates in the British House of Commons, or any other of the parliaments of Europe, will often have been struck by a very elementary fact. Many a question—be it tariffs, defence expenditure, economic aid, unemployment, the increased cost of living—presents problems which no one European parliament can resolve on its own. The solution involves the co-operation of the governments and the peoples of all the European countries. Today two-thirds of the matters which come before any of the parliaments of Europe raise problems which each individual parliament is incapable of solving on its own. They are matters of common concern to all the European peoples and the European parliaments and the European governments. They can only be dealt with properly, i.e. with real power, by a European parliament and a European government. The recognition of this necessity is a condition precedent to our recovery and our survival. Something of this was achieved for Great Britain some 250 years ago when Scotland, England and Wales were brought together by the Act of Union, and in this century this has to be achieved for the other areas of the world.

Independent separate sovereign states in the same continent or region are now out of date. Political organization from generation to generation may have to change to fit in with the new needs of the time. We want to develop and extend the area of government in the world. There is a central government in the Soviet Union. You might not like it, but it at least prevents war breaking out in an area which comprises one-sixth of the world. There is a government now in China, and one in India. There is one in North America. But there are continents or large parts of the world where there is not one. In Western Europe with 280 million people there are twenty countries. In Africa with 215 million people there are some twenty states. In South America with 110 million people there are seventeen states. 'To look for a continuation of harmony between a number of independent, unconnected sovereignties situated in the same neighbourhood (such as in Western Europe, in Africa, or in South America) is to disregard the uniform course of human advance and to set at defiance the accumulated experience of the ages.'[2] These words, without those in brackets, were written some 180 years ago. They are still true to-day.

If we are to have a world divided into a large number of democratic states each with its own separate systems of representative and responsible government, we will not have secured a democratic world. Democracy survives in the United States, not because that continent is divided into fifty states who all subscribe to the political theory of democracy and try to apply it, but because there is one government for the fifty states which has power over and above that of each of the states, and to which each of the states has surrendered some of its sovereignty.

Democracy will remain unstable as a political system so long as it is confined within the boundaries of individual small states. Leaving out of account the political systems which we envisage, there is no reason why the Soviet Union and the United States should not be stable countries and provide for their peoples a good standard of living and a community in which they can live their lives in peace. This is not true of other areas of the world. The states of Europe must surrender some of their sovereignty to a supra-national authority which will be able to exercise certain powers for Europe as a whole. The states of Africa must surrender some of their sovereignty to a supra-national authority which will be able to exercise certain powers for Africa as a whole. The states of Latin America must surrender some of their sovereignty to a supra-national authority which will be able to exercise certain powers for South America as a whole. And the states of Arabia and those of South East Asia must surrender some of their sovereignty to a supra-national authority which will be able to exercise certain powers for the different territories as a whole.

It may be said that a democratic government cannot be secured for the world, however much it may be desired. But, if that is so, there is no reason why the area of government cannot be extended where the extension will be most profitable, so as to obtain larger areas of government as the first step. The United States is already governing an area as large as Europe and providing law and order for 170 million people. In the same way the U.S.S.R. is a government extending over a very large territory and covering a population of nearly 200 million people. If a Government of Western Europe were established, if the twenty-six European states, including Great Britain, would create a United States of Europe, then there would be a government for another large area and for another large population. Instead of twenty-six tariff barriers in Europe there would be a single European government and a free trading market for the people all over the Continent. Instead of twenty-six armies, navies and air forces, there would be one European army, navy and air force. In short, instead of twenty-six democracies—even if so many could be established—all unstable because they could not solve their economic and political problems, there would be one European democracy, which like the democratic United States would have sufficient power to deal with the greater part of its economic and social problems.

A federal, political democracy like the United States may become an economic democracy. A federal and economic democracy like the Soviet Union may become a political democracy. In Europe, without federalism, both economic and political democracy will probably perish. In Latin America we are faced with the problem of creating both a democratic system of government in the political sense and an economic democracy as well, but neither can be secured without there being some form of common political authority for South America as a whole. The same problem has to be faced in Africa. It is not only a question of securing freedom for the colonial peoples and the right to govern themselves; what is of equal importance is to secure a common government for Africa which can develop the resources of that great continent, not in twenty different compartments, but rationally and for the benefit of the African peoples as a whole. We do not want to repeat in Africa the mistake made over the centuries in Europe.

The task of our time is to develop and extend the machinery of democracy in all its forms, political, economic and federal. However, since we have a reasonable amount of political democracy, and the field of economic democracy is daily being greatly widened, the time has come to concentrate on the creation and establishment of a machinery of federal democracy in those areas of the world where it does not exist. If we were to consider preparing a blueprint for the political organization for the world we would probably provide different levels. The smallest unit would be that of local government—the city government, or the council area, or the district, or whatever form of local government is to be found in the different parts of the world. Its powers would be limited and defined. Next in the order of ascendency would be the government of the state, which again would deal with matters of common concern to all the local governments in the area, but which are peculiar only to those local governments—questions of education and matters of that kind. Next we would come to some kind of government of a continental nature, whose powers, again, would be limited and defined, but which would have control of those matters of common concern—such as defence, customs and currency—which, so long as they are dealt with by the individual countries in each continental area, prevent full economic development, promote economic nationalism, and ultimately, as the past has shown, lead to war.

Consideration must be given to the matters of common concern which should be dealt with by a continental or regional authority, and what their competence should be. There are plenty of precedents to guide us in this investigation. The Congress of the United States has certain defined powers, so too has the Supreme Soviet under the Russian constitution. There are obviously a limited number of matters which should come within the competence of a regional authority, and the number of matters is limited because they must be matters upon which there is agreement between the individual peoples who comprise the citizens of the regional authority. It would be absurd to join the peoples of the Soviet Union and the peoples of Europe in one common authority, because there is no common factor of agreement between them as to what democracy means. Any definition of human rights would mean one thing to the Russians and another to the

Europeans. But if we are to create a political authority in Western Europe there would be certain fundamental human rights which are in common agreement among the European peoples, and which they would all accept as the basis of their constitution.

The Americans in creating their federal constitution adopted as a series of amendments at the outset their Bill of Rights. This was intended to define the rights of individual American citizens, and to protect those citizens against the encroachment of the political power. But it did more than this; for it defined those matters of a political nature in respect of which there was general agreement amongst the people of the thirteen states—the highest common factor of agreement in the principles of democracy, if you like. These ideas have been considerably developed since the end of the eighteenth century when the Bill of Rights was formulated. The United Nations has already drafted a Treaty of Human Rights, though as yet it is not operative; the Council of Europe has also adopted the European Convention on Human Rights and Fundamental Freedoms, which has now been ratified by all the member states except France. If we are to create a political authority in Europe, or in Africa, or in Latin America, in South East Asia or in Arabia, some principles must be acceptable to each of the peoples in those areas on what the structure of the political authority will rest. The draft Treaty of Human Rights would form a very good basis for a European constitution. If, for example, racial equality is one of the principles to be accepted in drafting an African constitution, then either South Africa will not join the African union, or, if she does, then the Federal Government of Africa will see to it that the principles of racial equality are enforced in South Africa.

The maintenance of law and order must be the second matter of common concern which any regional authority must have power to deal with, and in this connection we are at once confronted with the problem of the strategic places of the world, and where their control is to lie. Hong Kong, obviously, would go to China; Singapore would go to whatever political authority there might be for South East Asia; Gibraltar, Cyprus and Malta would become part of Europe. Difficulties might arise over such waterways as the Panama Canal, the Suez Canal and the Dardenelles, and it might be that these waterways would have to be placed under some international control to which the regional authorities were parties.

A number of economic matters will become matters of common concern. The creation of a common currency in each region and the abolition of all trade barriers, are without any question essential to the development of any regional authority. The United States has a common currency, and for all practical purposes there is a common currency in the whole of North America; so too is there a common currency in India, in China, and in the Soviet Union. It would be expected that the creation of any regional political authority for Europe, for South America, for Africa, or for Arabia would immediately bring about the creation of a common currency in those areas and the abolition of all barriers to trade between the states which formed part of the political authority. The very creation of the political authorities would in itself solve many of the problems with which the world is confronted at the present time. Trade would become a matter between the ten areas in the world, and would in all probability be limited to an exchange of raw materials, foodstuffs and capital goods.

Federation is a method of political organization which tries to establish a political authority whose business it is to deal with warmongers personally. It is a means whereby the instruments of warfare are taken out of the hands of warmongers and out of the hands of national states. A federation of Western Europe with Britain as a part would prevent any Nazi revival in Germany and any repetition of the Second World War. Federation thus is a method which establishes elementary order in the original or the international field. It does for states what the state did for individuals when it put an end to the settlement of personal disputes by the knife, the bottle, the bludgeon or the pistol. The more this kind of elementary order is established in the world the more can we talk about the social services, the welfare state and the development of essential progress, and not until. World federation being premature, let us start with the creation of a federation in those regions or continents of the world where a number of small states are contiguous with one another, so as to reduce the possibilities of war in that region or continent, and to extend the area of democratic government. The peoples in one state of the Soviet Union do not arm against the peoples of another state; nor do the peoples in one state of the United States arm against the peoples in another. But the peoples in one state of Europe arm against the peoples in another state of Europe; the peoples in the states of Latin America arm against the peoples of other Latin American states. For the solution is a political one. It is not to be found at the national level.

Democracy is, and must remain, an unstable form of government so long as it is applied to an area which is limited in population and in resources. Eighty independent sovereign states, each a law unto itself, and unwilling to admit the sovereign power of a higher authority, cannot without substantial sacrifice develop a democratic world or regional community. The division of Europe into twenty-six political units, each of different strength, and the barriers they created between themselves, was all part of the inflation in Germany in 1924, the economic depression of 1929, the unemployment in Italy and in Germany in 1931, the breakdown of democratic government, and the rise of dictators. For democracy as a form of government in twenty-six separate sovereign states will never survive. The economic and political nationalism which results from the full exercise of sovereign powers inevitably undermines the system of government in each individual state. Economic nationalism is a cause of unemployment, and unemployment in a continent like Western Europe cannot be cured in one state in isolation from the others. For Europe is an economic unity, and must be regarded as such. The problems of the European peoples can only be solved by a government for the region as a whole; under twenty-six different authorities their problems will only be aggravated. Thus Europe divided into many states, as it was prior to the last war and after it, can never have a permanent political organization. World War II was the inevitable result of the failure of the statesmen to recognize the need for the political unification of the Continent. Hitler, at least, acted realistically in unifying Europe, and treating it as a political and economic whole. What the democratic governments of Europe were unable to secure by agreement, he obtained by force. The only alternative to Hitler's New Order is not a return to the Europe of twenty-six independent sovereign states, as the Atlantic Charter suggested and the victors have determined since 1945, but to go forward to one democratic government for Western Europe as a whole.

The continent of Europe [said the future American Secretary of State during the Second World War] has been the world's greatest fire hazard. This has long been recognized, but it has seemed impractical to do anything about it. Now the whole structure is consumed in flames. We condemn those who started and spread the fire, but this does not mean that, when the time comes to rebuild, we should reproduce a demonstrated firetrap . . . from a purely selfish standpoint any American program for peace must seek some form of federation of continental Europe.[3]

CHAPTER 5

The Locust Years, 1945–59

'*There is a tide in the affairs of men,*
Which, taken at the flood, leads on to fortune;
Omitted, all the voyage of their life
Is bound in shallows and in miseries.
On such a full sea are we now afloat;
And we must take the current when it serves,
Or lose our ventures.'

William Shakespeare,
Julius Caesar, Act IV, Scene 3.

THE fifteen years after the Second World War have certainly witnessed a wide development in European integration, which some people will regard, despite its many setbacks and failures, as remarkable, though anyone regarding it objectively will come to the conclusion that with the exception of the 'Little Six' no real progress has been made at all. European integration means the integration of the countries in Western Europe, including Great Britain, and though many organizations have been brought into being, no effective political authority has been created except the Coal and Steel Community, the Common Market, and Euratom.

In this chapter we will review firstly the organizations which have been created over the last fourteen years; secondly the attitude which Great Britain has taken to each of the organizations when they were created; and thirdly the need for simplification of the existing institutions, which is becoming apparent to the governments and parliaments of most countries in Western Europe. A full description of the European institutions created since the war will be found in a book recently published by Dr. A. H. Robertson entitled *European Institutions*, which not only gives a chapter to each of the institutions which have been created, but contains in its Appendix the documents creating them. [1]

(i) Institutions Created Since 1945

The creation of European institutions started with the Treaty of Dunkirk concluded on the 4th March 1947, between France and the United Kingdom, to which we will refer subsequently, but immediately after the treaty was signed the Ministers went to the meeting of the Foreign Ministers in Moscow to settle a peace treaty with Germany, and it was the breakdown of those negotiations that brought the beginning of the 'cold war' and the end of any prospects of collaboration between the West and the Soviet Union. The breakdown of these negotiations was followed by Mr. Marshall's speech at Harvard in which he invited the European countries to draw up a recovery programme for which he promised American financial assistance, and as a result the Convention for European Economic Co-operation was signed in April 1948. The main purpose of the organization created by this convention was to administer the European Recovery Programme as previously prepared by the member governments in Western Europe, and to deal with the millions of dollars which the United States was giving to the European countries, on condition that there was a continuous effort on the part of the participating countries to achieve a common programme of recovery.[2]

Thus O.E.E.C. was created. It dealt with the administration of American aid, and has also played no small part in liberating the trade of the countries of Western Europe, and considerably increased the financial stability of the European countries by the creation of the European Payments Union, which, unfortunately, with the development of the Common Market, no longer exists. But it must be made quite clear that this organization was a co-operative one; all decisions were to be made by governments; and any resolutions of the executive committee had to be unanimous. The most, in effect, that O.E.E.C. could do was to make recommendations which the individual governments carried out; there was no transfer of sovereignty, or integration in any sense. It was an international organization for a limited number of countries, and it differed from the other principal European organizations such as the Council of Europe, the Coal and Steel Community and Western European Union, in so far as it had no parliamentary assembly. It was, in short, a purely intergovernmental organization.

The next development was the creation of the North Atlantic Treaty signed on the 4th April 1949. After the Dunkirk Treaty had been entered into in March 1947, this treaty was extended by the Brussels Treaty of March 1948, to include Benelux. The first of these, the Dunkirk Treaty, was entered into in order to prevent any further German aggression. The Brussels Treaty was prompted more by the continued menace of Soviet expansion. When the United States Senate adopted the Vanden-berg Resolution in June 1948, which affirmed American determination to exercise the right of individual or collective self-defence under Article 51 of the United Nations Charter, and which recommended that the United States should associate with other countries in arrangements for regional defence based on self-help and mutual aid, negotiations were started with the five Brussels Treaty powers and the United States and Canada which led to the signature of the N.A.T.O. Treaty in April 1949.[3]

Although the N.A.T.O. Treaty contains provisions for the further development of friendly relations and economic co-operation between the nations parties to it, it is primarily designed to provide for collaboration in self-defence; and in the ten years of N.A.T.O.'s existence there has been little, if any, collaboration in economic, social and cultural matters despite the provisions of the treaty. But there has been considerable co-operation between the powers in setting up a defence organization under a single supreme commander (General Eisenhower at first), who established his military headquarters near Paris, which is now known as the Supreme Headquarters Allied Powers Europe (S.H.A.P.E.).

The question has been raised on many occasions as to whether N.A.T.O. is going to be the growing point for something more compre-hensive, and if so, what? Despite the meetings of N.A.T.O. parlia-mentarians and particularly the Atlantic Congress held in London in 1959, nothing effective has been done to foster the idea of an Atlantic community. N.A.T.O. may have played a substantial part in the last ten years in preventing further Russian aggression, such as took place in Czechoslovakia, but to the eyes of many people both behind the Iron Curtain and in the neutral countries it is little other than an anti-Commun-ist bloc. Over the ten years repeated efforts have been made from time to time to develop the non-military side of N.A.T.O., and in 1956 three Ministers—'the three wise men'—were appointed to make recommenda-tions indicating how this could be done, and they made their report in respect of which no radical action has as yet been taken. The essence of their proposals was that there should be developed and strengthened political consultation between the member countries. While, in their view, the need for military co-operation was as great as ever, security was far more than a purely military matter; for while political and economic co-operation also was essential, the military co-operation would never succeed if the other co-operation was not made effective. So far, the views of the 'wise men' have not penetrated very far. N.A.T.O. is purely a military organization led by the United States. It is little more than the focus of the organization of Western Europe against Soviet aggression.

The Council of Europe was created by statute a month after the creation of N.A.T.O., by the Brussels Treaty powers, and as a result of the movement for European unity which had developed after the Hague Congress. The aim of the Council of Europe according to its first Article is: 'To achieve a greater unity (in the French version "union") between its members for the purpose of safeguarding and realizing the ideals and principles which are their common heritage and facilitating their economic and social progress.'[4] The continental members of the Brussels Treaty powers desired a legislative assembly, but Britain was opposed to such an assembly, though willing to join some organization where the power lay in a Committee of Ministers at government level. The result was a compromise which set up the Council of Europe with a membership of most of the countries of Western Europe, since increased to sixteen, with a Committee of Ministers and a Consultative Assembly. At its meeting in September 1949 the Consultative Assembly of the Council of Europe was asked by the Committee of Ministers to consider any change in the political structure of Europe necessary to achieve a greater degree of unity between the members of the Council of Europe. In response to this request the Assembly unanimously resolved that the aim of the Council of Europe was: 'The creation of a political authority with limited functions but real powers.' No progress was made in any development along these lines. The Council of Europe has remained a debating chamber, which, although it has created many committees and suggested many Conventions, has done little other than to bring together and educate a large number of politicians from the countries of Western Europe and to formulate on many major questions a European opinion, which, because of the lack of executive power, has been quite ineffective. Early in its history the Council of Europe split into two groups: those who wished to see a political authority with limited functions but real powers, the Benelux countries, France, Germany and Italy; and the remainder who wished to see the organization functioning only at government level without a legislative assembly. The result was that the Little Six finally decided to advance on their own, and this led to the creation of the first effective political organization in a part of Western Europe.

In 1950 M. Robert Schuman, French Minister for Foreign Affairs, proposed that a convention should be entered into for a supra-national authority covering coal and iron and steel in Western Europe, and several countries were invited to take part in a conference to study his proposals. The British Government felt itself unable to participate in the negotiations, as it would not accept the basic proposals put forward by the French, namely that the Community would ultimately lead to a federation of Western Europe; and that it should have an independent High Authority which could exercise power if necessary without the approval of the individual governments. Six countries, the Federal Republic of Germany, France, Italy, and the Benelux countries accepted, and the result was the treaty to create a European Coal and Steel Community which was ratified in 1952.[5] The treaty provides for a High Authority which is an executive body and which administers the Coal and Steel Community; a special Council of Ministers which has powers set out in the treaty; a Court of Justice, which has jurisdiction to hear certain classes of appeals against the High Authority; and finally a Common Assembly which discusses the reports submitted by the Authority, and has power to approve or reject them, which, in fact, gives it power to overthrow the High Authority and put another one in its place should it so desire.

As a result of the developments of N.A.T.O. and of the Coal and Steel Community, and the desire of the United States to rearm Germany, negotiations took place to create a European Defence Community on similar lines to the Coal and Steel Community and finally a treaty was agreed between the six powers in May 1952. This treaty provided for a Common Assembly, and the question arose as to whether there should be two assemblies for the same group of countries or only one. As a result of this discussion the Common Assembly of the Coal and Steel Community was instructed to produce a draft treaty for a European Political Community. This was prepared by a committee of the Assembly, and subsequently (May 1953) adopted by the Assembly. This treaty contains detailed provisions for a European parliament of a federal character consisting of a People's Chamber with 268 members, and a Senate of 87, representing the states. The French Parliament rejected the European Defence Community, and as the Americans and British wanted Western Germany to rearm, some other method had to be devised. Finally, it was agreed that the six powers, parties to E.D.C., together with Britain, should amend the Brussels Treaty and create a new organization, Western European Union. This provides the terms and conditions on which the members should maintain their military forces on the Continent in peacetime, and puts them under the command of the Supreme Commander, N.A.T.O. The purpose of W.E.U. was twofold: first to provide for the rearmament of Germany and its admission to N.A.T.O., which it has done; second to supervise the European Statute of the Saar, but this second object never became necessary as the referendum in the Saar rejected the Statute by a majority vote.[6]

Critics of European institutions can wonder why W.E.U. has continued to exist as a separate organization. It has a Council of Ministers which meets in London, and an Assembly similar to the other assemblies of the Little Six which meets in Paris; but in fact it serves merely as the nucleus of the seven Western European countries meeting within the framework of N.A.T.O., and it can have no defence policy separate from that of N.A.T.O. Like most bodies of its kind, it has created a number of committees, and is really duplicating the work already done either by

N.A.T.O., by the Council of Europe, or by the Coal and Steel Community; and the cynic may well ask whether it serves any purpose other than to educate Members of Parliament from its member countries in matters of European defence. It certainly has no executive power, and it would be difficult to find any case where it has had any influence over any of the recent political developments in Western Europe.

The last of the major institutions created since the war are the European Economic Community and Euratom. These probably are the most important developments which have taken place; and again they are limited to the Little Six (the three Benelux countries, the Federal Republic of Germany, France and Italy). Britain and others were asked to join in the talks at Messina which led to the Treaty of Rome, which created the European Economic Community, but refused to take part under the mistaken impression the European Common Market would be rejected by the French Parliament as had been the E.D.C. The purpose of the treaty is to create a Common Market over the next twelve to fifteen years for the six countries, so as to provide for the free movement of goods, agriculture, persons, services and capital, and transport. Like the Coal and Steel Community, the treaty provides for a Council of Ministers to ensure the co-ordination of the economic policies of the member states, and to make effective decisions without reference back to national governments. In addition, there is a Court of Justice, a Development Fund, and provision for many other organizations. Since the treaty was signed, as the members of the Coal and Steel Community, the Common Market, and Euratom are the same, the bodies have agreed upon a Common Assembly now known as the European Parliament, so there has been an element of simplification in the institutions which the Little Six have created.[7] A table showing the existing European institutions and their membership is shown on p. 103.

In addition to the six organizations already described, nine further organizations have been created; five of these are technical, and four are more of a political or geographical character. The technical organizations are: the European Conference of Ministers of Transport; the European Civil Aviation Conference; the Conference of Posts and Telecommunications; the Customs Co-operation Council; and the European Organization for Nuclear Research. All these bodies have arisen partly as a result of the discussions in the Council of Europe, and of the meetings of Ministers in the post-war period, and there is a real need for the rationalization or streamlining or simplification of these organizations within one of the other bodies which already exist. The smaller organizations comprise the Rhine Commission, which is limited to the specific problem of the administration of the Rhine; the Benelux Economic Union, which is an attempt to bring together in one customs union Holland, Belgium and Luxembourg,

Table showing the Membership of European Organizations[8]

	OEEC (1)	C. of Europe	NATO (2)	ECSC	WEU	Econ. Community	Euratom	ECMT	ECAC	CCC (4)	CERN	Rhine Com'n (5)	Benelux	Nordic Council	Balkan Alliance
Austria ..	X	X						X	X	X	X				
Belgium ..	X	X	X	X	X	X	X	X	X	X	X	X	X		
Denmark ..	X	X	X					X	X	X	X			X	
Finland ..														X	
France ..	X	X	X	X	X	X	X	X	X	X	X	X			
Germany ..	X	X	X	X	X	X	X	X	X	X	X	X			
Greece ..	X	X	X					X	X	X	X				X
Iceland ..	X	X	X						X	X				X	
Ireland ..	X	X							X	X	X				
Italy ..	X	X	X	X	X	X	X	X	X	X	X				
Luxembourg ..	X	X	X	X	X	X	X	X	X	X			X		
Netherlands ..	X	X	X	X	X	X	X	X	X	X	X	X	X		
Norway ..	X	X	X					X	X	X	X			X	
Portugal ..	X		X					X	X	X					
Spain ..	X							X	X	X					
Sweden ..	X	X						X	X	X	X			X	
Switzerland ..	X							X	X	X	X	X			
Turkey ..	X	X	X					X	X	X	X				X
United Kingdom ..	X	X	X		X			X	X	X	X	X			
Yugoslavia ..	(1)							X	(3)		X				X

For key turn to Note 8, page 146.

but which, in due course, must merge its identity with the Common Market; the Nordic Council, which is an inter-governmental body like the Council of Europe or Western European Union, with a parliamentary body made up of representatives from Denmark, Finland, Iceland, Norway and Sweden. This body was not created by treaty, but by identical laws being adopted in each of the parliaments of the member countries, but there is no international obligation of a legal nature on the part of any of the states, and any one country can repeal the law creating the Nordic Council in its own country, and cease to be a member. Finally, the last of the organizations is the one creating the Balkan Alliance which has arisen out of a series of treaties between Greece, Turkey and Yugoslavia, and it is a treaty of alliance, political co-operation and mutual friendship. A further treaty which established the Balkan Consultative Assembly was signed in Ankara in 1955, and this largely follows the precedents set up by the Council of Europe, the Coal and Steel Community, the Nordic Council, and Western European Union, by associating with their work representative delegations from the different national parliaments.[9]

(ii) Britain's Wasted Opportunities: 1945–59

The British attitude to O.E.E.C. is very easy to understand. When Mr. Marshall made his famous speech at Harvard, Mr. Bevin lost no time in responding, because of his determination to base British foreign policy on an Anglo-American alliance, or full co-operation with the United States. Mr. Bevin as a member of the War Cabinet in 1940 had known what it was for his country to stand alone, and he was determined thereafter to follow a policy which, if at all possible, would continually tie the United States at least to Britain, if not to the continent of Europe. It was very largely this conception that prevented him from being seriously interested in the development of post-war Europe, except with America playing the leading part. As was pointed out at the time, the offer of Marshall Aid would have been of much greater service to the countries of Europe if it had been made as an offer to one European authority instead of to fifteen. Experience has shown, as many people said at the time, that the granting of aid by America to the individual countries was going to increase the economic nationalism of those countries, and this has certainly been borne out by the developments which have taken place in the Benelux countries, France and elsewhere. Every one of the Acts of Parliament passed by Congress, either for Marshall Aid or for Mutual Aid which succeeded it, has contained either in recitals or in the operative part of the Act words to the effect that America is a prosperous country because she has a Common Market with a large population, with one political authority, and that Europe could be equally prosperous if it would only unite in the same way. To the politicians on Capitol Hill, Marshall Aid was meant to unite Europe under one political authority; but Mr. Bevin would have none of that. He and his British colleagues were clever enough to see that the grants from the United States under Marshall Aid were made to the individual states without the creation of any common authority; and the Americans were too polite to interfere and dictate the conditions on which the gift would be made and received. The great opportunity of the post-war world was missed in 1948, for if such a European council had been created then, with real power, and the grants from America had been made as block grants to be administered by such a European council, the foundation of a Western European federation would have been laid.

When one comes to examine many of the items which came to Europe under Marshall Aid, we see that a large number were totally unnecessary. Many millions of dollars were used by the United States to supply freight cars to France and Italy. These freight cars could have been made in Britain or Switzerland or Sweden and could have been supplied to France and Italy from any one of those three countries; but if they had been made in any one of the three countries they could not have been bought by France or Italy because the French and Italian governments had not sufficient foreign exchange to buy them. In the case of Britain insufficient sterling, in the case of Switzerland insufficient Swiss francs, in the case of Sweden insufficient Swedish kronor. What was wrong in Europe was not that it needed freight cars from America, but that it needed a common currency so that the peoples of Western Europe could trade with one another. No manufacturer in Birmingham is prevented from selling to the people of Scotland because they are short of sterling. There is no archaic currency barrier between England, Scotland and Wales such as exists between the fifteen countries of Western Europe; nor has the development of the United States been hindered because people in Texas or California cannot manufacture and sell to the people of the eastern states of America because of a shortage of foreign currency, as all the people in the fifty states trade in dollars in all their transactions. So long as Europe permits the obstacle to trade of twenty different currencies, twenty different customs barriers, twenty different quota systems, twenty different types of subsidies, so long will the productivity of Europe remain much less than that of the United States. Marshall Aid was intended to increase the productivity of Europe, and though it did succeed in doing so to a certain extent, it could have succeeded to a much greater extent if it had not been made available in a way which perpetuated and increased the existing archaic barriers of currency and trade. It should have insisted on steps being taken to have those barriers removed and it should have insisted on the money being administered by one European authority. However, when O.E.E.C. was created this was not the British attitude. The British Government saw a chance to secure aid which would help to prolong the independent position which Britain was trying to maintain, and the opportunity was lost to bring about the integration of the European countries, which was so greatly desired.

The second organization which was created, namely N.A.T.O., is in keeping with the British policy of associating with the United States. Under Article 2 the parties agreed to contribute towards the further development of peaceful and friendly international relations by:

(*a*) strengthening their free institutions;
(*b*) bringing about a better understanding on the principles on which these institutions are founded;
(*c*) promoting conditions of stability and well-being;
(*d*) eliminating conflict in their international economic policies;
(*e*) encouraging economic collaboration between any or all of them.[10]

Although the treaty has been in existence for ten years, nothing has been done under any one of these five headings, as is becoming more and more apparent. The N.A.T.O. Treaty is merely a military alliance— an anti-Communist bloc created by the Atlantic and Western European countries. It is entirely under the control of the United States, who completely determine the policy which N.A.T.O. follows. It is quite unrepresentative of the people of Western Europe and serves to indicate the dependence of this country and the other countries of Western Europe on the United States.

Over the years there have been criticisms of N.A.T.O. by the neutral countries, Austria, Ireland, Sweden and Switzerland, who are anxious to avoid any connection with N.A.T.O. because of its direction, and also by those who, while welcoming the Atlantic Alliance for defence purposes, believe that European unity is an independent necessity whose successful development would be endangered if it were associated too closely with the Atlantic Alliance. 'We must not drown Europe in the Atlantic,' was a phrase used by many people who took this view, and in the debates in Strasbourg several members have raised the whole question of this sort of alliance.[11] Mr. Costello from Ireland, for example, said: 'By all means let us ask the American and Canadian parliamentarians to assist in our debates, but before building an Atlantic community let us first build a European one; both would perish if we tried to do both together.'[12] In the same debate Mr. Bohy of Belgium said: 'I never made any secret of my friendship with the United States nor of my desire to be independent of it. I want to be allied to the United States and I truly believe that in the present international situation the freedom of Europe depends on the alliance with the United States. But I hope this will be a real alliance, by which I mean one based on equality. . . . This equality can only be attained when an equivalent European union can take its place behind the United States.'[13] This, of course, has never been the view of the British Government, and it is because Britain has always turned her back on Europe and looked towards North America and the Atlantic community that she has been unwilling to give any real attention to the question of the integration of Western Europe.

It is now common knowledge that no British Government has ever genuinely been interested in the Council of Europe; that they would have preferred that the continental brain-child was either still-born or strangled at its birth; and that if Mr. Bevin could have had his way with the other Brussels Treaty powers he would not have had any Assembly at all, much less a Consultative Assembly, though he was prepared for a Committee of Ministers to meet from time to time. Lord Strang, who was Permanent Under-Secretary at the British Foreign Office at the time, has described Mr. Bevin's firm hostility to the whole idea and the trouble to which he went to make the Council of Europe 'as little embarrassing as possible to the United Kingdom'.[14] Despite this, Mr. Bevin had earlier led people to think that he believed in European union. Speaking in the House of Commons in January 1948 he said:

> But surely all these developments which I have been describing point to the conclusion that the free nations of Western Europe must now draw closely together. How much these countries have in common. Our sacrifices in the war, our hatred of injustice and oppression, our Parliamentary democracy, our striving for economic rights and our conception and love of liberty are common among us all. Our British approach, of which my Rt. Hon. Friend, the Prime Minister, spoke recently, is based on principles which also appeal deeply to the overwhelming mass of the people of Western Europe. I believe the time is ripe for a consolidation of Western Europe.[14A]

Earl Attlee, who was Prime Minister of Great Britain at the time the Council of Europe was formed, has given expression to his views on the subject in his autobiography, *As It Happened*, where he writes:

> The Brussels Treaty and the Atlantic Pact were both designed to strengthen and to unify the Western democracies. They were a recognition of the fact of the changed balance of power in the world. It is hard for those whose memories go back to the nineteenth century to realize that Western Europe, so long the dominant factor in the world, is today a collection of disunited elements lying between two great continental Powers—the U.S.A. and the U.S.S.R. Germany

is potentially a great Power, but France is unlikely ever to occupy again the position she once held. A realization of this has created a demand for some form of federation, but there is a general recognition that without Britain such a grouping would not be strong enough to hold its own. On the other hand, Britain has never regarded itself as just a European Power. Her interests are world-wide. She is the heart of a great Commonwealth and tends to look out-wards from Europe though maintaining a close interest in all that goes on in that Continent. Indeed, the advent of air power has made her connection with the Continent a greater necessity than in the days of naval power when splendid isolation was a possible policy. As a general proposition it is obvious that a closer association of the West European States is desirable; indeed, I am on record as having said, 'Europe must federate or perish,' but to bring such ideas into the region of the practical is a very difficult proposition. Every State has its old traditions and its special ideological set-up. Some of our American friends did not always realize this. They did not appreciate the difference between European federation of old-established communities and the federation of the 13 American Colonies.[15]

Anyone who was a delegate to the Council of Europe from Britain knows how very little real interest was taken in the Council of Europe by the British Government of the day. Unfortunately, it became rather a matter of party politics, as the Conservative Party who were in opposition gave it great support, and therefore the Labour Government took the opposite view. Subsequently, when the Conservative Government took office in 1951, people on the Continent thought at last full support would be given by the British Government to the Council of Europe; but again they have been disillusioned. For those who led the Conservative Party when in opposition in 1949–50 and gave full support to the Council of Europe, and are now the foremost Ministers in the British Government, have shown little interest in it since 1951, as the speech of the Lord Chancellor indicated to the Assembly in 1951.[16] Moreover, it is interesting to note that the Labour Party now in opposition have taken much more interest in the Council than they ever did when they were the British Government, and that the leader of the Labour Party delegation to Strasbourg became the President of the Assembly. Nevertheless, the charge remains true that the Council of Europe, and its development and its success, has been spoilt by being made a plaything of party politics in Great Britain, and this is only one other aspect of the way in which Britain has wasted its opportunities to bring the European peoples together.

At the Council of Europe, particularly in 1949, all the delegates from the European countries looked to the British delegation for a lead which they never received, and finally, in their disappointment, those of the Little Six turned away from the Council of Europe and created a smaller but more effective organization of their own. In other words, they decided to create an authority with limited functions but real powers even though

it extended only to the Six. When M. Schuman first made his proposals
about the Coal and Steel Community they were issued as a White Paper
in Great Britain, and a debate took place about them in the House of
Commons. In his proposals M. Schuman indicated that he hoped the
Coal and Steel Community would serve as the foundation for a federation
of Western Europe, and it was because of the presence of this sentence
that the British Government refused to accept the invitation to participate
in the conference to discuss the matter. In the debate which took place,
Sir Stafford Cripps gave the reasons for the Government's refusal to
participate.[17] He pointed out that as the coal production of Great Britain
was twice as much as that of the whole of the other countries invited, and
as the steel production of Great Britain was half as much as that of the
other countries invited, the matter was of considerable concern to this
country. But his main objection was that, while Britain was prepared
to join some European organizations, she was not prepared to participate
in them without knowing the details of the proposals to which she would
be committed. He gave as an illustration the negotiations with the European Payments Union when the Convention which created it set out in
detail its functions, its powers, the obligations of members, and the way
in which it was to operate. Moreover, speaking in the debate on the
Schuman Plan, Sir Stafford Cripps, referring to the method of negotiating
the European Payments Union, said: 'This negotiation is, I think, typical
of what can be accomplished by a freely negotiated agreement between
governments. I am perfectly certain that if in this case some supra-national
body had attempted to impose upon us by a majority vote some payments
scheme without any prior discussion between governments, it could only
have resulted in a complete failure, and in our having to leave the organization.'[18]

If the British Government had approached the Council of Europe on
those lines, as we shall see when we come to consider the Strasbourg
Protocol, that method of negotiation could easily have been applied, but
when the amendment of the statute was proposed to give effect to a
proposal on those lines, the British Government still refused to co-operate.
The Dutch went to the conference on the Schuman Plan but reserved
their rights with regard to being bound to consider any kind of a political
federation for Western Europe. In the debate, Sir Winston Churchill
suggested that the British Government might take the same attitude; and
of course they could easily have been present at the conference, taken
part in the negotiations, and, following the lines outlined by Sir Stafford
Cripps in his speech, only accepted the proposals when satisfied that the
draft Treaty for the Community was satisfactory to them. It is difficult
to acquit the British Government of the charges of hypocrisy and perfidy
that have been laid against them in regard to their policy in Europe over

the post-war years; for, despite all their protests about their interest in Europe, in fact they have refused to take advantage of any opportunity offered for any real and effective integration of Western Europe.

The last of the main developments in the post-war years are the Common Market and Euratom, which resulted from negotiations started at Messina, and which led to the execution of the Rome Treaty. Britain again was one of the countries invited to the Messina Conference, and on this occasion it was a Conservative and not a Labour party that was in power, but once more the British Government refused to attend. At the time the invitation was issued over one hundred Conservative Members of Parliament and almost as many Labour Members of Parliament put down two Motions in the House of Commons giving support to Britain attending the Messina Conference. These resolutions were as follows:

That this House expresses agreement in principle on the establishment by stages of a common market in Western Europe and urges Her Majesty's Government to accept the invitation to participate in the negotiations currently taking place on the subject between the representatives of Belgium, France, the Federal Republic of Germany, Italy and the Netherlands, with a view to ensuring that if, or when, any treaty is signed the way will be open for British participation in the common market on an acceptable basis and in accordance with the interests of the Commonwealth and Empire. (Conservative)[19A]

That this House, while recognizing that there would be both advantages and disadvantages for this country in membership of the proposed common market, and that it would be necessary for the United Kingdom, as for each other country, to seek appropriate compensating concessions for the risks and sacrifices involved (such as Imperial Preference), nonetheless urges Her Majesty's Government to accept the invitation to participate in the negotiations among the other six member countries of Western European Union and endeavour to negotiate arrangements which would make it possible for the United Kingdom to participate in the advance towards a common market without detriment to the interests of the Commonwealth. (Labour)[19B]

It is very difficult to understand why the British Government would not even go to this conference to discuss the question of a Common Market. Obviously the economic relationship between Great Britain and the other Commonwealth countries and the territories of the Colonial Empire are matters which make her position somewhat different from that of the other countries, excepting France. Nevertheless, as studies have shown during the discussion of the Free Trade Area, Commonwealth trade is not a real objection to our joining the Common Market, as seven-eighths of it would hardly be affected by our joining the Common Market, and it should not have been very difficult to make satisfactory arrangements with regard to the remaining one-eighth. As we shall see in the next chapter, the Commonwealth has been used as an argument against Britain playing her proper part in Europe, when in reality the Commonwealth does not stand in the way at all. The real reason lies in Britain's determination not to give up any part of her sovereignty and to associate not with the countries of Western Europe but with the United States. After her refusal to attend the Messina talks the Common Market came into being, much to the surprise of the British Government. Though I have not seen the cables despatched by the British Ambassadors in the countries of the Little Six, I am certain that when the archives of the Foreign Office are opened to the public, they will show that our ambassadors advised the British Government against participating in the Messina talks, because they thought the Treaty of Rome would never be ratified, and the Common Market would never become a reality. As in the case of Cuba, of Egypt, and of so many other countries, the British Government have been completely misled by their representatives abroad in regard to the sensible position to be adopted, or if they have not been misled, they have refused to take the advice tendered. Either interpretation is evidence of expensive incompetence.

The Rome Treaty having been ratified, negotiations then proceeded with the other countries of O.E.E.C., certainly under British leadership, to bring about a Free Trade Area; but to the objective observer it must be quite obvious that if the British and Scandinavian countries were not prepared to take part in the talks in Messina it was very unlikely that the countries of the Little Six would agree to modify what they had already done in order to join the other countries of O.E.E.C. in a Free Trade Area, limited only to industrial products as was proposed. Obviously, Britain wanted the best of both worlds. She wanted to keep her Commonwealth preferences; she wanted to keep an open market for agriculture; and yet she wanted to have the benefits of selling her manufactured goods in the area of the Common Market. Thus it is that Britain's refusal to participate fully in the negotiations which were going on has resulted in the creation of the Common Market limited only to the Little Six, with seven of the remaining countries of O.E.E.C. creating a loose, peripheral Free Trade Association for themselves, which at worst only divides Europe further and at best makes no positive contribution to the integration of Western Europe as a whole.

(iii) The Simplification of the European Institutions

Dr. A. H. Robertson in his book on *European Institutions* has devoted a chapter to this subject, and in the course of it he writes:

It was not unnatural that during the decade from 1948 to 1957 European co-operation took on so many different forms. On the contrary it was a healthy sign. This was a period of evolution and experiment; different methods were tried out and different forms of co-operation put to the test. Some were purely inter-governmental, while others contained parliamentary organs; some were limited geographically to six or seven countries, while others included fifteen or more. At the beginning, this was no bad thing. After ten years, however, the time for stocktaking had come, and it was necessary to put a little more order and system into the heterogeneous collection of European Institutions which had grown up over the last decade.[20]

Obviously the need for some kind of simplification is long overdue, and there are many reasons for it. First, when the treaties for the Common Market and Euratom came to be discussed, it appeared that there would be two more institutions with Committees of Ministers and Assemblies. However, as a result of the discussions which took place, a considerable measure of simplification of the institutions of the three six-power communities was achieved. They now have only one European Parliamentary Assembly, and not three; and it was natural that people should consider that the simplification which they had secured should be applied to the other European organizations. In the second place, there was duplication between the Council of Europe and Western European Union, as the latter organization has not confined its activities to defence, but has inherited and developed the social and cultural programmes of the Brussels Treaty Organization which led to duplication and overlapping with the Council of Europe. In the third place, it has long been clear that the Council of Europe and O.E.E.C.* should merge. The Assembly of the Council of Europe has called for this merger on several occasions, but so far no such merger has taken place. In the fourth place, the signature of the Treaty of Rome led to a certain amount of stocktaking on the part of everybody; for it became obvious that the delegates to the European Parliament were going to devote more time and attention to the problems of the Little Six than to the problems of the Council of Europe, and in many places the question was asked as to whether the Council of Europe had not become redundant. This, in itself, has led to another reason for simplification. If European unity is to become a reality, it must have a large measure of support, and this means it must be something which the man in the street can understand. European institutions with their committees and overlapping organizations present a bewildering jungle of muddle to the people of Western Europe today, and do not do the cause of European unity any good whatsoever. To put the matter in the simplest

* Publisher's note: this book was written before the replacement of O.E.E.C. by O.E.C.D. was decided upon. Since O.E.C.D. includes Canada and the U.S.A. as full members, it clearly affects the proposal to merge O.E.E.C. with the Council of Europe, which is confined to European countries.

way, the Council of Europe has fifteen committees and twenty-five sub-committees, making forty in all. Western European Union has seven committees. The European Parliamentary Assembly has fourteen committees. The N.A.T.O. Parliamentarians' Conference has five, the Benelux Council has eight, and O.E.E.C. has ten, making at least eighty-four committees for these organizations, quite apart from the committees which have been created in some of the other organizations. The details of these committees can be seen from the table, pp. 114-15.[21]

Several things emerge from any examination of the institutions which exist. Obviously, it is only a matter of time before the Little Six will become completely one political authority for coal and steel, the Common Market and Euratom, with either a Committee of Ministers, or a Senate, as one political body, and an Assembly, ultimately elected, as the other. In the second place, before long we may hope to see O.E.E.C. and the Council of Europe merge. One then asks the question, what is the need for Western European Union at all? The principal reason for its creation was to strengthen the defences of Western Europe by reason of the failure of E.D.C. and to provide a way for the admission of Western Germany to N.A.T.O. This has been successfully achieved, and the defence work which it does could equally well be done by N.A.T.O. itself,* or by a committee of N.A.T.O. The second function was to supervise the European status of the Saar which the Franco-German Treaty of 1954 was intended to institute. However, this never came into existence as the referendum on the Saar was rejected. In the third place, W.E.U. has certain important functions to perform in relation to the armed forces of the member states of the continent of Europe, which is only another one of its defence objects which could equally well be handled either by S.H.A.P.E. or by one of the committees of N.A.T.O. Finally, there are the social and cultural aims of the Brussels Treaty which W.E.U. has inherited, and which could perfectly well be carried out by the Council of Europe.

We are, therefore, left with two groups; the Little Six as one organization; and the Council of Europe as another, absorbing O.E.E.C., W.E.U., the Conference of Ministers of Transport, the Civil Aviation Conference, the Customs Co-operation Council, the Organization for Nuclear Research, the Nordic Council, the Baltic Council and the rest. If this were done, we would then be left with two groups, the Council of Europe embodying co-operation in inter-governmental organization at government level, and the Little Six embodying the principle of real integration with a transfer of sovereignty to the political authorities which it creates. The real task of simplification or of rationalization is to merge these two concepts and

---

* Except in so far as the provisions of Article V of the amended Brussels Treaty, concerning automatic assistance in case of aggression, are more far-reaching than those of Article V of the North Atlantic Treaty.

Committees of European Assemblies and Organizations

Consultative Assembly Council of Europe	European Parliamentary Assembly	Western European Union	Nordic Council	Benelux Inter-parliamentary Council	NATO Parliamentarians' Conference	(Inter-governmental) O.E.E.C.
Bureau of the Assembly / Joint Committee / Standing Committee	Bureau	Bureau / Presidential Committee	Praesidium	Permanent Committee	Bureau and Standing Committee	Executive Committee
Political Committee	Political & Institutional Affairs Comm. / Sub-committee on Direct Elections	General Affairs Committee		External Affairs Committee	Political and Institutional Affairs Committee	Committees: / – Trade and Payments
Economic Committee	Commercial & Economic Co-operation Committee / Common Market Committee / Long-term Finance and Investment Committee		Economic and Transport Committee	Economic Committee / Fiscal and Customs Committee	Economic Committee	– Fiscal / – Economic / – Manpower / – Overseas Territories
Social Committee	Social Affairs Committee	Social Affairs Committee	Social Committee	Social Committee		Products Committees: / – Coal
Cultural Committee	Scientific and Technical Research Committee / Nuclear Energy Committee	Cultural Sub-committee (of General Affairs Committee)	Cultural Committee	Cultural Committee	Cultural and Information Committee / Scientific and Technical Committee	– Oil / – Electricity / – Gas / – Iron and Steel

Legal Committee	Legal and Rules Committee	Procedure and Privileges Committee	Legal Committee	Legal Committee	– Non-ferrous Metals – Timber – Chemical products – Pulp and Paper – Maritime Transport – Tourism
Rules and Procedure Committee	Health and Working Conditions Committee	Budget and Administrative Committee	*Ad hoc* Committees		
Budget Committee	Budget and Administrative Committee	Working Party for Liaison with National Parliaments			Nuclear Energy Committee
Working Party on Relations with National Parliaments					European Productivity Agency: – Productivity Committee – Applied Research Committee
Local Authorities Committee	Overseas Territories Committee				
Committee on Non-represented Nations	Transport Committee			Agriculture, Food Supply and Fishery Committee	Agriculture and Food Committee
Agriculture Committee	Agriculture Committee	Defence and Armaments Committee			
Population and Refugees Committee				Military Questions Committee	

these two groups of organizations together. The basic idea of a united Europe, as expressed at the Hague Congress in 1948, was that by uniting Europe would become a powerful force for peace in the world; that it would ensure its economic independence and social progress; and that in making a European community Europe would become an equal partner with the United States. It is for this reason that any simplification of European institutions should not take N.A.T.O. into account. But there is also a difficulty which must be faced, which is that Austria, Ireland, Sweden and Switzerland, being neutral countries, might not want to join in a European organization which had power to deal with matters of defence. Nevertheless, although they have proclaimed a policy of neutrality and have refused to have any association with N.A.T.O., it would be quite a different proposition for them to join a united Europe as one state, which would then, if it wanted to, make an alliance with the United States. There can be little doubt as to what is the task which faces the politicians of the countries of Western Europe and of Great Britain. The division between the Little Six and the rest of Western Europe cannot continue. For, while in the first instance the organizations may be reduced to two— the Little Six and the Council of Europe—we still have to bridge the gap between those two and create some kind of effective political authority for Western Europe as a whole by the integration of the Little Six with the Council of Europe.

CHAPTER 6

Britain and a United Europe

'Europe must federate or perish.'
Mr. Attlee, 1939

'Everybody cries: "A union is absolutely necessary," but when it comes to the manner and form of the union their weak noodles are perfectly distracted.'
Benjamin Franklin, 1758

'The Peace Settlement of 1919 collapsed, not because those who supported it were moved by ideals which were too exalted for practical politics, but because both the idealists and the practical politicians were thinking in terms of Sovereign States—terms which belonged to the Renaissance and were archaic in the twentieth century, exactly as the conception of a centralized Empire was obsolete in the ninth century. The history of the "Dark Ages", however, shows how difficult it is for any age to escape from the ghosts that haunt the graves of the past.'
Delisle Burns

THE idea of European union, or European unity, has been developed over many centuries, and since the Second World War every prominent statesman in Western Europe has given it some kind of support. They all agree on the need for European unity, but they do not define the Europe they are talking about, nor do they explain what they mean by the words unite, union, or unity. In the British text of the Statute of the Council of Europe, the aim of the Council is to achieve 'greater unity between its members'—but the French text refers to 'greater union between its members'—and both texts are equally authentic. It may sound strange to suggest that a union of countries can mean anything other than their coming together and merging their identity in respect of certain matters, but that is not the interpretation which the people of Britain have put upon the phrase. The American Union meant originally the bringing together under one government of thirteen states, though the states retained their powers in regard to certain matters; the Union of South Africa means the joining together of several countries. The differences which have arisen between Britain and her continental neighbours relate mostly to the way in which the union should operate.

Does European union mean co-operation by the governments of Western Europe at government level without any surrender or merger of their sovereignty in respect of any matters? Or does it mean a European parliament with a European government, and the surrender of sovereignty? This is the fundamental difference between the British and the Scandinavians on the one hand, and the French, Italians, Germans and the peoples of Benelux on the other. If the British want any association with the states of Western Europe at all, they want it limited to co-operation at government level; and if any political organization is necessary it should be allowed to grow piece by piece in respect of individual matters. The peoples on the Continent want a federal union and a constitution defining that union. Many people over the last few years have talked of European union without really contemplating political union in our time, and of a United States of Europe without meaning a federation at all; and there are those who advocate Western European union, but expect the states to retain in full the independence which they have enjoyed over the centuries.

But then a further difficulty arises. Does Western Europe mean only those countries on the Continent, or does it include Great Britain?

We must re-create the European family in a regional structure called, it may be, the United States of Europe. . . . In all this urgent work, France and Germany must take the lead together. Great Britain, the British Commonwealth of Nations, mighty America, and I trust Soviet Russia—for then indeed all would be well—must be the friends and sponsors of the new Europe and must champion its right to live and shine.[1]

That extract from Sir Winston Churchill's speech at Zurich shows clearly what most people have failed to understand. Sir Winston has never advocated a federation of Western Europe with Britain as one of the member states, though he did support the United Europe Movement, is a President of the European Movement, and has supported the Council of Europe, of which Great Britain is one of the original members. Ever since the war there has been confusion. Mr. Bevin's policy of Western Union certainly included Great Britain among the Western countries, and few people on the continent of Europe can be blamed if they did regard the European Movement as including Great Britain in the union of the continental countries. In the Brussels Treaty and the Statute of the Council of Europe Great Britain was one of the promoting countries. There is no need to haggle over the words 'unity' or 'union'. In view of the Russian threat to Western Europe and her control over Eastern Germany and the satellite states, any union of Western Europe today means an effective political union of the countries west of the Iron Curtain including Great Britain.

Let us therefore consider first the form of organization which needs to be created in Europe. We have already in the previous chapter examined briefly the different institutions created in Western Europe since the war and the British attitude to them. Having considered the form, then let us consider the case of Britain as part of Western Europe, and finally the case for European union—for the creation of the third Europe—and the great opportunity which the creation of such a union offers to the leadership of this country.

(i) The Manner and Form of the Union

In the last chapter we reviewed the institutions which have been created in Western Europe since the war, and indicated the confusion which exists on account of the multifarious organizations which have been created; their many committees and the overlapping which had taken place; and the urgent need for the simplification of all the institutions. We also argued that the British Government, either by its lack of interest, or real hostility to the idea, and by its refusal to co-operate effectively, has lost opportunities on many occasions that would have led to the integration of Western Europe, to the benefit of all the member countries. It is the argument of this chapter that the Council of Europe is the institution which should be used to absorb all the other institutions, but that its constitution should be changed to provide for an effective political authority. If we assume the need for the creation of an effective political organization, the question at once arises as to the manner and form of the organization which, as in 1758, has in the last fifteen years so distracted the weak noodles of so many otherwise eminent politicians. No one would argue that it would be practical politics today for the European states to draw up a constitution similar to that of the United States. For, after all, that constitution was prepared for thirteen small colonies of four million people, who had only just secured their independence, before the days of the Industrial Revolution, and at the end of the eighteenth century. Such a constitution would hardly be suitable for an area covering some twenty European powers (some of whom have been great powers and still think they are), comprising 280 million people, at a time not only after the Industrial Revolution, but in the age of mass production and automation, and 180 years later, in the second half of the twentieth century.

However, much thought has been given to the suitable form of organization for Western Europe, and during the last ten years two proposals have been made: one the Strasbourg Protocol, of 1950, for the basic amendment to the Statute of the Council of Europe, and the other the draft Treaty for the European Political Community which was prepared in 1953. It will be appreciated that the Strasbourg protocol which was intended to amend the Statute of the Council of Europe was based on the fifteen (now sixteen) states members of the Council of Europe. The draft statute for the European community was limited to the countries of Benelux, France, Western Germany and Italy. Nevertheless, the provisions of the draft statute could easily be amended to cover the whole sixteen countries of Western Europe. It is the argument of this section that either the protocol or the draft statute, with such amendments as may be necessary to bring them up to date, both provide a way to create an effective political authority for Western Europe, and we will consider each in turn.

The Strasbourg protocol dealt mainly with four questions: the merger of existing institutions; an elected Assembly; the rule-making power of the Assembly; and an executive council, i.e. an effective government for Europe. The proper starting point for any definition of Conventions is to consider the specific needs which have to be met. There are a few matters which, if they are to be handled with effect in Western Europe, must be treated as matters of common concern. In the economic field these imply the increase of production, the development of inter-state and external trade, the elimination of trade barriers, and ultimately a common currency. These economic matters are largely covered by O.E.E.C. and by the Brussels Organization at government level, and likewise in the field of defence by W.E.U. Thus, in the first place, the protocol provided that all the different European institutions should be merged; that instead of the many existing institutions there should be only one, with one Committee of Ministers and one Assembly; and that the aims of the Council of Europe should be extended so as to include all the matters covered by O.E.E.C. and the Brussels Treaty and the other organizations that were in existence at the time. This would now be extended to bring in Western European Union, the Coal and Steel Community, the Common Market, Euratom, defence and the other institutions of Western Europe created since the war discussed in the last chapter.

In the second place, the protocol converted the Consultative Assembly into a proper European parliament, and a parliament in which through one of its houses, the governments would have the final say. Such a conception met the British requirement of action at government level, but it also met the continental desire for the creation of a proper parliamentary authority. Under the protocol the Council of Europe becomes a parliament of two houses: the Committee of Ministers as the Upper House representing governments; and the Assembly as the Lower House nominated at first by the parliaments of the member states, but ultimately being directly elected by the people and representative of and responsible to them. Since the protocol was considered by the Assembly at Strasbourg a European Assembly Bill has been drafted, which would provide for the direct election of members to the Assembly of the Council of Europe using the existing constituencies in the sixteen countries of Western Europe.

If the formula for the development of the Council of Europe is to be a compromise between the Little Six and the rest, as it must be, then the need for unity at government level is recognized by the proposal which invests the final authority of the Council of Europe in the Upper House, or Committee of Ministers. The continental members of the Council of Europe want a European parliament which is representative of the peoples of Europe, and not one like the United Nations, where delegates are nominated by governments. The British and Scandinavians have been opposed to any European parliament in the accepted sense, i.e. one with power to legislate and act. On the other hand the British Government has made it quite clear that they are not opposed in principle to the creation of supra-national authorities in Europe provided the details of the powers of the authorities are worked out in advance. As the Government said in the House of Commons: 'We are not standing out all the time against the creation of any supra-national authority: all we are saying is that we must know the extent to which we are being committed before we agree to the surrender of any of our sovereignty to a supra-national authority.'[2]

The proposals in the protocol were specifically designed to meet this official statement of policy, and it provides authority for the Assembly to make rules in the nature of treaties or conventions, which once passed by the Assembly and the Upper House would confer power on the Council of Europe and define the limits within which they could exercise authority. If the protocol had been adopted the treaty for the creation of the Coal and Steel Community, for the Common Market, for Euratom and for the European Defence Community, could all have been dealt with by the Assembly of the Council of Europe in this way. For the machinery set out in the protocol provides both for the initiative to come either from the Assembly or from the Committee of Ministers, and for freely negotiated agreements between governments to be converted into powers of the Council of Europe.

Under the protocol, the Council of Europe has no legislative power delegated to it in advance; any powers are given to it strictly *ad hoc*, for a particular and agreed subject. If, however, this proposal had been adopted, the Assembly would have ceased passing resolutions of disputed competence, but would have seen its competence widen automatically as new subjects were deemed in turn to be suitable for its rule-making powers. In this way the Council of Europe would have the right to pass European laws, but although no law would. be passed without the consent of each individual government, the power and prestige of the Council of Europe would automatically increase in proportion to the tasks and functions assigned to it. As M. Spaak wrote of the protocol at the time: 'The Assembly will only acquire and develop the powers which it will be granted in proportion to the competence assigned to it by the passing of each European law. A theoretical definition is no longer necessary; each practical instance will provide part of the solution.'[3]

The last proposal of the Protocol provides for the creation of an executive council, small in numbers but responsible to both houses. This would take the place of the present standing committee of the Assembly, but would become, in time, a European cabinet or government. Such an executive council would meet regularly; it would organize the agenda of the Assembly; it would prepare its legislation; and control the whole of the administration of the Council, including the direction of those organizations brought within the scope of the Council of Europe by the incorporration of the many different institutions created in Western Europe since the war. In time, departments would be created for individual matters, such as defence, customs, finance, trade, agriculture, production, social services, transport and legal questions. Once a bill had been passed by both houses of the Council of Europe, the executive council would, of course, be entrusted with the duty of giving effect to the bill. In this way, over a period of years, a European government could grow up.

At the time when the protocol was under consideration, the Chairman of the Special Committee, Sir David Maxwell Fyfe (now Lord Kilmuir), and the writer, as Rapporteur, wrote a letter which was published in *The Times* summarising shortly what the protocol could do for Europe and recommending its acceptance by Great Britain. This letter was in the following terms:[4]

Sir,
    Shortage of space is, no doubt, responsible for scant attention being paid by the British Press to the Protocol for amending the Statute of the Council of Europe, which was described at some length by Monsieur Spaak, as Chairman of the Assembly, at a Press conference in Brussels on Monday last. In view of the great significance of the proposals as a compromise solution to much sterile argument, and their potential significance to future British policy, we should be grateful for space to make a brief explanation of them. . . . The Protocol, if adopted, will provide something more than co-operation at Government level,

as exists at present in, for instance, the Council of the Organization for European Economic Co-operation, but something less than the kind of supra-national authority which has always been opposed by the British Government. We believe that the difficulties of the Council of Europe have been greatly increased by the transfer—both by its critics and its friends—of the terminology of different centuries and circumstances. We therefore ask you to let us describe the essence of the procedure put forward by the committee.

This is that no powers should be ceded in advance to the Council of Europe. It is only when all Governments have agreed that a concrete proposal is a proper subject of united action that powers will be given to carry that proposal into effect. The normal pattern of working would be that the Assembly should devote itself to evolving practical and detailed measures instead of merely to resolutions. When a measure comes to the Committee of Ministers the Governments through their representatives would say whether in their view this was a subject for united action or not. If they took the view that it was, then they would evolve the highest common factor of agreement and undertake to give effect thereto. So far as the Council of Europe is concerned the Committee of Ministers would be in a position analogous to that of a second chamber. So far as the Governments are concerned, it would be a permanent treaty-making machinery in which complete liberty of action and the requirement of unanimity would be preserved. Nevertheless, both committee and Governments would be rightly subject to the pressure of informed European opinion on the desirability of the united action proposed.

The other aspect is to remove some of the duplication in international agencies by letting an executive authority of the Council of Europe responsible to both the Committee of Ministers and the Assembly take care of those organizations which already exist under the O.E.E.C. convention. In the future the same authority would also take care of other international organizations created by the procedure outlined above. Defence would no longer be removed from the scope of the Council of Europe. It is not suggested, of course, that this Protocol is incapable of further amendment and improvement. But it does, at least, provide the possibility of the emergence of that political authority 'with limited functions but real powers' which is the unanimous aim of the Assembly. Nor should it be necessary to stress the relevance of these proposals to present-day defence problems and the appointment of General Eisenhower. It is plain enough that the closer integration of Europe is coming inevitably owing to the needs of defence: that is beyond argument. The old dilemmas are disappearing; all that remains as the choice for this country is whether we are to have a European authority created by Western Europe itself, under the guidance of Great Britain, or whether we are to have one imposed from outside.

Since the protocol was rejected Europe has split into two groups, as we saw in the last chapter: the Little Six who formed first the Coal and Steel Community and now the Common Market and Euratom; and the remaining countries of O.E.E.C. Now the latter, after the failure of the Free Trade Area negotiations, are floundering around not knowing what to do. Their course is clear: first, to join the Common Market and have an effective Free Trade Area in Western Europe; second, to simplify or rationalise the existing institutions in Western Europe; and third, to create a European political authority on the lines of the protocol or the statute for a European community, which satisfies the requirements of both groups. No doubt many changes would have to be made in the texts in the light of the experience of the past ten years. Probably the unanimity rule in the Committee of Ministers would have to go; and perhaps the Upper House might have to be enlarged and the members nominated by their respective governments. These, however, are questions of degree and detail, and not of principle. The solution to the dilemma of Western Europe is a political and not an economic one, and only some development along the lines of the protocol or the statute will provide such a political solution.

At the end of 1951 and the beginning of 1952 after the E.D.C. Treaty had been signed, the Foreign Ministers of the Six invited the Common Assembly to draft a statute for a European Political Community without waiting for that treaty to be ratified. A treaty to create a European Political Community was drafted and adopted by the Common Assembly, though, as the E.D.C. Treaty was not ratified, it has, of course, never become effective. Nevertheless, it provides a guide for the type of political organization suitable for Western Europe, for, although it only relates to the Benelux countries, France, Western Germany and Italy, it could be adapted to provide a constitution for the whole sixteen members of the Council of Europe. In some ways the provisions of the draft treaty are different from those of the protocol. It provides for two Houses of Parliament: the People's Chamber, to be elected, and the number of Deputies from each member state is provided; and a Senate to be nominated by the national parliaments, and the number of Senators for member states also is provided. Provision is made also for an executive council, for a court, and for certain specialized authorities.

But the powers of the draft statute are very wide. It not only provides for the integration of the European Coal and Steel Community, which would now include the Common Market and Euratom, and the defence community, but it also gives the community certain powers in international relations and economic matters which would enable the community to develop as an effective authority for Western Europe, with limited functions but very real powers. The draft treaty for the European community satisfies the requirements of the Little Six, and there is little reason why it should not also be accepted by the other nine countries of Western Europe. If only Britain and the remaining countries of Western Europe could just make the little effort—one spasm of resolve—to join the Common Market, a draft treaty for the creation of a European political authority would not be difficult to work out; for the Council of Europe and the other European assemblies over the last ten years provide sufficient material for a constitution, or the form, of the European organization to be determined.

(ii) Britain, the Commonwealth and Western Europe

The view expressed by a large number of people when the question of Britain and Europe is raised always runs along the lines that Britain is a part of three groups in the world, the Commonwealth, the Atlantic community, and Europe, and that we must continue to remain in each. In the debate in the House of Commons on the Common Market and the Free Trade Area, the Prime Minister, Mr. Harold Macmillan, said:

Whenever we are faced with the type of problem which we are to discuss today, we are conscious of three distinct forces working upon us. We in this island are founder-members of the great community with which we all feel the strongest of ties, and that community is of great importance to all of us in our daily lives. No small part of our own economic and financial strength and that of our partners depends upon our association with the various countries, independent and dependent, within the British Commonwealth. And, even stronger than these most material interests, are, of course, deep emotional bonds. That is our first problem.

Then, secondly, we are European geographically and culturally, and we cannot, even if we would, dissociate ourselves from Europe. We are moved by the continued efforts in the post-war world to strengthen the unity and cohesion of the old world.

Thirdly, we are members of a great alliance which itself links across the Atlantic the old world and the new, and we can never be unmindful of any of these three forces at work upon us. Politically and economically we must, of course, continue our searching for a course of action which, while serving the vital domestic interests of the people of this island, would enable us to play our part in strengthening Europe as an integral part of the whole free world. At the same time, we must fortify and strengthen our Commonwealth links.[5]

Nor is his view very different from the Labour view, for a statement on foreign policy issued by the Labour Party in 1952 states:

The Labour Party firmly believes that the survival of Europe must depend on closer unity between its peoples. If Britain is to play a full part in building European unity, it must be based on co-operation between Governments working together by mutual consent. This we have done in respect of the O.E.E.C. and the E.P.U. and we are willing to consult on other useful forms of co-operation between Governments. But Britain could not join a European federation or a European customs union. We must safeguard our freedom to play a full part as an independent member in the Commonwealth and the Atlantic community. Moreover, we cannot surrender to any supra-national authority the right to determine British policy on such vital matters as full employment and fair shares.

The Labour Party recognizes, however, that some European countries may wish to form a closer union than Britain herself could join. In that case Britain should place no obstacle in their path, and should seek the closest possible association with whatever union they form.

Nevertheless the Labour Party is convinced that Western Europe, with or without Britain, and however close its unity, cannot stand alone in the modern world. European unity is possible only within the context of the wider Atlantic community. Any form of European unity which might tend to weaken the Atlantic community is to be avoided. For this reason the Labour Party would oppose Britain joining a European army separate from N.A.T.O. unless the United States and Canada were also prepared to join.

It is strange how difficult it is for the leaders of our time to escape from what Mr. Delisle Burns calls 'the ghosts that haunt the graves of the past', and how impossible it seems for them to escape from conceptions which, if they once had a meaning, have none today! If there is an alliance which links itself across the Atlantic between the old and the new world, it is not an alliance between Britain and America, but one between Europe and America. We often hear people talking about our cousins across the seas, without ever realizing that, in the main, the American cousins are cousins of Europeans chiefly, because the greater part of the immigration to the United States came from the countries on the continent of Europe, despite the number that went from the United Kingdom and Ireland. Furthermore, such opinion as exists in the United States on the subject of Britain's role in the world, always supports Britain as part of Western Europe. The United States looks not for an alliance with Britain, but on the contrary hopes that Britain will play her proper part in strengthening the political structure of Western Europe. For the people of the United States would much prefer to have an alliance with a United States of Western Europe, of which Britain formed a part, than to have to deal, as she must at the present time, with sixteen different and very independent European countries.

As to the first point, while it may be true that we are founder-members of the great community which is now the Commonwealth, it is hardly true to say that our economic and political strength depends upon our association with the countries of the Commonwealth. The question has been fully discussed in Chapter 2, where it was made quite clear that the future of the Commonwealth is one of disintegration. The colonial territories in Africa will probably work out their own future in their own way

as part of Africa; Canada, Australia and New Zealand will draw nearer to the United States; India and South East Asia will become quite independent of the other white dominions; so that finally Britain will be left as an island on her own off the coast of Europe, and no longer the centre of a great Commonwealth.

The need for Britain to associate with Europe comes not only from the desire, which was—and still is—strong on the part of the Europeans, that Britain should associate with them in the creation of a European federation. It arises primarily, because only by such an association can Britain resolve her economic and political problems. We need Europe as much as, if not more than, Europe needs us. For, without the creation of some kind of European federation, there is no end to the recurrence of economic crises in Great Britain, whatever the politicians, be they Conservative or Labour, may try to say. Nor is this position confined only to Britain. It applies to the other countries of Western Europe too. For there is no happy future for any small country either politically or economically: politicially because it cannot defend itself without external help (and that certainly applies to Britain); and economically because a decent living-standard means higher real wages, increased productivity and more raw materials. None of these can this country provide on its own. Thus there are very powerful political and economic arguments for encouraging the union of Britain with the countries of Western Europe. A strong Western Europe with a sense of unity and purpose is an important link in the free world, and the schemes for economic integration have come to play an important role in the European search for unity. We should, therefore, do everything to encourage the Common Market by joining it, and not impede its development. If we impede its development we shall certainly be regarded by Europeans and by Americans as well, and with some justice, as being a serious obstacle to the growth of strength and unity in the free world. As we shall see, most of the arguments against Britain joining the Common Market are raised on the grounds that it threatens Imperial Preference, but, as Professor Meade has pointed out, 'there are still some bitter memories, particularly on the part of the peoples on the Continent, of the way in which by claiming our full most favoured nation rights under our then existing commercial agreements, we killed the Ouchy Agreement for the gradual reduction of tariffs in the Low Countries in the 1930's, but simultaneously built up our own preference system at Ottawa. This is an issue on which the Continental Europeans and Americans would be exceptionally sensitive.'[6]

But there are certain very good political reasons why we should join the Common Market. In the first place, this is the initial step towards a more closely unified Europe, and a closely unified Europe associated with the United States would do very much to bring about stability in the world. In the second place, we have to face the German problem, and we do not want Germany either to dominate Western Europe, which she will do if Britain is not a part of it, or to go on her own in the way in which she did in the early part of this century. Without Britain playing her full part in association with the other European countries, how can the problem of Germany be solved? Twice in this century Germany has plunged the continent of Europe into war. The only way to solve the German problem is to create a political union of Western Europe, of which both Britain and Germany form a part, and to impose permanently on the Germans only those sacrifices of sovereignty which we are prepared to impose on ourselves. Does the British policy convince those who have suffered German occupation that everything is being done to prevent the revival of German nationalism? If German strength is needed to supplement the defence potential of the West, how can this be obtained without a revival of German nationalism?

One of the chief problems with Germany is to direct German power into peaceful channels. European union would do this by absorbing her bodily into a new and larger political system—a system including Britain. Without Britain it would not be large enough to ensure that Germany would not eventually dominate it. It is small consolation to those who support the Coal and Steel Community, the Common Market, or Euratom, to know that Britain merely approves these projects. They still fear German domination; and they are still reluctant to encourage the full participation of Germany in the defence of the West. The issue so far as Britain is concerned turns on her interpretation of the place which Britain can take in the world. Is Britain strong enough, and is the Commonwealth of sufficient importance to warrant her assuming that she is a first-class power, and that she can stand on her own feet without association with the states of Western Europe? Is M. Spaak not right in insisting that only as a state of Europe is there a future for Great Britain? Is the free world to be built on two pillars—Western Europe (of which Great Britain forms a part), and the United States—or on three—Western Europe, the British Commonwealth and the United States?

Great Britain has a manufacturing capacity today greater than that which the export markets of the world can easily absorb on the basis of the present-day trading situation. We cannot guarantee to sell abroad our increased exports as things are. A free market in Europe, with its large population of 280 million people, would enable the British manufacturer to sell his present output and in future years to increase his turnover. Only in this way can we get the benefit of mass production and standardization with lower costs of production and bring about lower prices and higher real wages. This applies to most of the manufacturers in Great Britain, and to the manufacturers in the other countries of Western Europe too. If the

European market were one, the demand of a big market, such as stimulates the manufacturer in Detroit and Chicago, would stimulate the manufacturer in Manchester, Birmingham and Coventry, Rouen, Milan and the other industrial cities on this side of the Iron Curtain.

By joining the Common Market and pushing forward the further economic integration of Western Europe we will no doubt encourage the Scandinavian countries, and some of the other countries of Western Europe, to follow our lead and to take part in it; for so far they have been holding off because we were not prepared to participate to any extent. But, as we have already said, the primary reason for Britain to join the Common Market is her own self-interest. Only recently, in one of the Bulletins for Industry issued by the Treasury, British exporters were urged to concentrate more on selling to North America and Western Europe, and to concentrate less on selling to the easier and more protected colonial and Commonwealth markets on which many of them have been increasingly depending.[7] Government economic experts, analysing post-war trends in the world trade, came to the significant conclusion that the reason why Britain's share of world trade had been falling, while the share of other countries like the United States and Germany had been rising, was that Britain has been concerned too much in selling to the primary producing countries and too little to the manufacturing countries.

'Figures for post-war trade,' so the *Treasury Bulletin* observes, 'show clearly that while trade between manufacturing countries and primary producing countries (i.e. countries selling mostly food or raw materials) has increased 38 per cent since 1948, trade between the manufacturing countries themselves has increased much more strikingly by 57 per cent. This is explained by the broad generalization that in recent years the richer countries have been increasing their wealth faster than the poor countries, and their people have been spending a smaller proportion of their new wealth on food and natural raw materials and a larger proportion on manufactured consumer goods, on machinery and on synthetic, manufactured materials. This is particularly true of West Europeans.

Indeed, the *Bulletin* makes the assertion—which should please Washington—that 'the main force behind the rising volume of world trade has been the recovery and growing prosperity of the Continent of Europe. . . . The story of the change in pattern of world trade is the story of the economic recovery of Europe.' The *Bulletin* concludes that

it would be dangerous to our future prospects, therefore, to assume that the Continent of Europe is not our market but Germany's; in the last six years the European market has expanded much more than the sterling area, and it seems likely to do so again in 1955. If we are to finance our rising import bill we must take every opportunity of expanding our share of the growing markets for manufactured goods among which, if present trends continue, North America and

Western Europe are likely to show the most rapid rates of increase. We must be flexible enough to move with expanding markets quickly and not merely to wait for prospects in our traditional markets to improve.[7]

If that were true in 1955 it is even more true today.

Coming from an official source, such an outspoken caveat as this against Empire trade is not likely to be very welcome in some sections of the Conservative Party. Equally, it may not be very palatable to those on the political Left who have always argued that Britain's economic future lay in becoming the workshop for the under-developed continents. The unpleasant truth seems to be emerging that self-interest and the brotherhood of man may not pull in the same directions. Other unpleasant truths conveyed in the same *Bulletin* are that British labour costs are still rising, both absolutely and per unit of output; and (by implication) that investment cuts would do serious harm to the upward trend of industrial output. For the figures show that industrial output rises by £37 for every extra £100 spent by consumers, and by £83 for every £100 spent on investment.

No doubt, however, people will continue to argue that it is impossible for us to join the Common Market because of Imperial Preference and our trade relations with the other Commonwealth countries. This was the line taken by the Prime Minister in the speech already referred to, when he pointed out that:

If the United Kingdom were to join such a Customs Union the United Kingdom tariff would be swept aside and would be replaced by this single common tariff. That would mean that goods coming into the United Kingdom from the Commonwealth, including the Colonies, would have to pay duty at the same rate as goods coming from any other third country not a member of the Customs Union, while goods from the Customs Union would enter free.

Judged only by the most limited United Kingdom interests, such an arrangement would be wholly disadvantageous. We could not expect the countries of the Commonwealth to continue to give preferential treatment to our exports to them if we had to charge them full duty on their exports to us. Apart from that, our interests and responsibilities are much wider. I do not believe that this House would ever agree to our entering arrangements which, as a matter of principle, would prevent our treating the great range of imports from the Commonwealth at least as favourably as those from the European countries.

So this objection, even if there were no other, would be quite fatal to any proposal that the United Kingdom should seek to take part in a European common market by joining a Customs Union. I think that we are all agreed there. I feel sure that the Governments of the countries who are negotiating their Customs Union in Brussels understand and appreciate our position in this matter. So that is out.[8]

Here is a further illustration of the way in which ideas, which may have been effective in the past, have absolutely no relation to the circumstances of Britain's position today. And it is rather odd that the British Government should go out of its way to urge the impossibility of joining the Common Market on the ground of Imperial Preference and Commonwealth trade, when any short review of the position shows, in the first place, that the whole system of Imperial Preference is on the way out and will certainly end before the period of ten to twelve years which is the period provided for in the Common Market for securing uniform tariffs; and, in the second place, that very little Commonwealth trade should be affected were Britain to enter the Common Market—less than one-eighth, which is not very great.

Britain has two tariffs, one general, and the other the preferential tariff which applies to imports from the Commonwealth. The Six intend, eventually, to adopt a single common tariff by averaging the French, German, Italian and Benelux tariff levels. If the United Kingdom were to accept the principle of a common tariff, it would add its own tariff as a fifth factor in the averaging process, and the influence of other European tariffs might be included as well, since the Scandinavians, Austrians and Swiss would also be likely to join. Therefore what matters to the United Kingdom is the difference between the two British tariffs and the proposed common tariff of the Six. As far as the United Kingdom general tariff on materials and manufactures is concerned, it appears to be remarkably similar to that of the Six; in fact, closer than any single one of the four existing tariffs of the Six themselves. Thus, the adoption of a common tariff will present very few problems in this case. Britain's general tariff on foodstuffs is lower than that which the Six are likely to have, and harmonization would, therefore, require substantial adjustments.However, Mr. Maudling said in the Free Trade Area debate in the House of Commons that he was 'confident that, could we solve the broad problems, a suitable agreement on agriculture, satisfactory to both the House and our European neighbours, could be found'.[9] It should not be unduly difficult to reach such agreement on agriculture, within the framework of the common system of managed markets proposed for the Common Market. The United Kingdom general tariff, therefore, presents no great difficulties.

Let us now look at the question of Imperial Preference, and in doing so we follow very closely the most illuminating report on this subject published by Federal Union, *Britain in the Common Market—The Implications for Commonwealth Trade*. The tariff on imports of most items from the Commonwealth is zero. The Six will not accept this zero tariff in a single European market. The French, in particular, insist that it would result in diversions of trade through the United Kingdom into the Six, whatever precautions may be taken by using certificates of origin; and they also claim that the effect of tariff-free competition from the Commonwealth in the United Kingdom market would be to keep United

Kingdom costs, in certain industries, down to levels which would consti-
tute unfair competition from their point of view. On the assumption that
these views must be accepted, what, then, would be the effect of replacing
the United Kingdom preferential tariff by a common European tariff?
How far could special arrangements be devised to avoid any adverse
effects on Commonwealth exports to the United Kingdom? As far back
as February 1957, the *Economist*, commenting on the Free Trade Area,
was writing: 'The more one examines the tariff schedules concerned, the
more convinced one becomes that the tying of this decision to the need to
maintain Imperial Preference is mainly a red herring.' Over one-half of
United Kingdom imports from the Commonwealth consists of food,
drink and tobacco which, as Mr. Maudling suggested, can be fitted in
with the agricultural proposals of the Common Market. Another quarter
consists of materials for industry, such as rubber, wool, cotton, copper
and tin, on which the Six, as well as the United Kingdom, levy no tariffs,
and on which the common tariff would, therefore, also be zero. The
remaining quarter consists of manufactures and certain raw materials.
Special measures seem fairly easy to devise in order to safeguard the
Commonwealth position as regards commodities accounting for about
half the value of this trade. Aluminium, lead, zinc, wood and wood products are the most important of them. Thus, as the Federal Union report
points out, seven-eighths of British imports from the Commonwealth
provide no obstacle to Britain joining the Common Market as the following table shows:

United Kingdom Imports from the Commonwealth[10]
1956

	£ million	per cent
Food, drink and tobacco ...	844	53
Materials on which United Kingdom and Com- mon Market tariffs zero ...	356	23
Materials for which special arrangements can be easily devised ...	180	11
Other materials and manufactures ...	215	13
	1595	100

Only one-eighth of the trade remains to be considered, consisting of
manufactures and of minor raw materials, and with regard to these, special
arrangements for the more important manufactures could be made with
the other member countries. In the Treaty of Rome provision is made for
the free entry into the Common Market of imports from Eastern into
Western Germany, so that the precedent for the solution of one-eighth of
our trade already exists. If special arrangements for our minor imports

cannot be negotiated then we must revise the tariff arrangements stemming from the Ottawa Agreements; and as has already been pointed out the Ottawa arrangements have already been revised in part with respect to New Zealand, and will have to be revised further during the next few years.

As the Federal Union report concludes: 'Britain is faced with a clear choice. Either we refuse to accept the principle of Common Market membership, and thus renounce the possibility of participating in the single European market; in this case the growth of our economy, and hence of all our imports from the Commonwealth, will be retarded. Or else we join the Common Market, and allow the resulting forces of economic growth to work in full upon seven-eighths of our imports from the Commonwealth. Even if there were to be no special compensation for the damage to the remaining eighth of the trade, this would clearly be the best course for the Commonwealth as for ourselves. But on joining the Common Market we will be able to get special compensation for Commonwealth countries, in the form of suitable kinds of assistance from the whole Common Market. It may, at first, appear surprising that the advantages for the Commonwealth should lie so overwhelmingly on the side of our joining the Common Market; but there is, in fact, a single powerful reason for it. If we stay outside, we will be politically and economically weak. If we go in, not only will our own strength be enhanced, but we will have the whole weight of Europe behind policies designed to develop the countries of the Commonwealth.'[11]

Opinion is changing slowly. Early in 1959 the sixth unofficial Commonwealth Conference was held in New Zealand and the New Zealanders sponsored a resolution for a closer association of Britain with Europe. During 1958 on several occasions the New Zealand Government were discontented with the way the discussions on the Free Trade Area were progressing and wanted to participate in them. Most people in the Commonwealth countries want Britain to join in Europe and do not believe that her joining would necessarily weaken the Commonwealth economic system. In fact they think, as the resolutions at that conference show, that it would strengthen it. Why then does Britain hold back?[12]

In the light of this examination it is difficult to follow the reasoning of the British Government on this issue. Speaking at The Hague, on 10th June 1959, Mr. Maudling reiterated that a Free Trade Area was still the best method of organizing European economic co-operation, and that it was up to the Common Market countries to come forward with alternative proposals, and he continued:

In the meanwhile, time does not stand still. While there have been no dramatic developments, it is quite clear that the present situation throws considerable strain on the Organization for European Economic Co-operation and on European economic unity. There is a widespread feeling in the United Kingdom that our trade with our friends in the Netherlands, and in other countries of the Six, is now seriously threatened. This is a development which must give cause for concern to all of us who believe in the cause of European unity.

There can be no question of Britain joining the Common Market countries. The community cannot be extended to include Britain and the other countries without a fundamental revision of the Rome Treaty. I do not see a general desire among the members of the community for such a revision. In any case there are other political and economic problems which would make it impossible. It has been suggested that there should be a negotiation between the United Kingdom and Commonwealth and the community; this suggestion does not, on examination, present any practicable solution.

We have, therefore, rejected these two suggestions. We are pursuing the possibility of a free trade area among seven European countries. The reasons for this are simple. We still believe in the long run that something akin to a free trade area is the right solution for Western Europe. We wish to see a multilateral non-discriminatory association between the Six and the rest.[13]

The Free Trade Area is dead, and only one-eighth of British trade would be affected by the Common Market. The institutions of the Treaty of Rome and the treaty itself are not objectionable as we have seen, and any development of the Seven can only serve to divide Europe even more. The Maudling case is most misleading, as Mr. T. Balogh has recently shown, and there is no fundamental reason why Britain should not join the Common Market: only prejudice.[14]

The Common Market Treaty contains provisions inviting other European states to join, so we may assume that if the British offered to join the offer would be accepted, and a serious British proposal to join the community might transform the situation by bringing a great body of reasonable European opinion over to the British side. 'The proposal would not, of course,' as the *Economist* has pointed out, 'have to be so heavily hedged about with conditions that Britain would once more be open to the charge of seeking to obtain the benefits without paying the fee.'[15] To make it would involve some major decisions.

Britain would have to be ready to accept all the features of the Common Market that are essential to its character as an economic institution; the institutional set-up, the investment fund and rehabilitation fund, the free movement of capital and labour, and the harmonization of social charges notably equal pay for women, as provided for by the Rome Treaty. There is nothing here that obviously rules out a British proposal to join. Concerted economic policies, free movement of the factors of production—even, perhaps, funds to overcome regional difficulties—were implicit in the Free Trade Area if it was going to work. More distrusted in this country than these economic proposals are the feared political implications of the authority exercised by the institutions of the Common Market. But there is no insuperable objection here either.[16]

The Commonwealth objection is in reality a bogy. We have refused to join the Common Market on political and not on economic grounds, for we do not want to give up the independent position which we have maintained for so long. But, today, there is only one logical new approach for Britain: to join the Common Market; to join a broader association of the countries of Western Europe; and to negotiate in a way satisfactory both to Europe and to the Commonwealth countries such adjustments as can be made so that each can fully enjoy the markets of the other.

(iii) One Spasm of Resolve!

A united Europe—the third Europe—means peace between the nations of Europe, and also peace between the social classes. This means providing well-being for the ordinary people of Europe.

What confronts us today [writes Professor R. H. Tawney], is not merely the old story of the rivalries of ambitious nations, or the too familiar struggles of discordant economic interests. It is the collapse of two great structures of thought and government, which for long held men's allegiance, but which now have broken down. The first is the system of independent national states, each claiming full sovereignty against every other. The second is an economic system which takes as its premise that every group and individual shall be free to grab what they can get, and hold what they can grab. Those methods of organizing the affairs of mankind may be admired or detested, but two facts are incontestable. In the past they worked, though with endless waste and ill will; they now work no longer. The result is the anarchy, international and economic, which threatens to overwhelm us.[17]

It will be noticed that Professor Tawney puts the breakdown of the independent national states first, leaving the economic system in a secondary position. In other words, he emphasizes the need for the creation of a political structure in which the countries of Western Europe will be states, and without this structure no other really effective economic integration or development can take place.

Professor Arnold Toynbee, in an essay on *The Dwarfing of Europe*, raises this question in another way. He points out that, before the First World War, Europe enjoyed an undisputed ascendancy in the world and that the special form of civilization which she had built up for herself was in the process of becoming world-wide:

Yet this position, brilliant though it was, was not merely unprecedented and recent; it was also insecure. It was insecure chiefly because, at the very time when European expansion was approaching its climax, the foundations of West European civilization had been broken up and the great deeps loosed by the release and emergence of two elemental forces in European social life—the forces of industrialism and democracy, which were brought into a merely temporary and unstable equilibrium by the formula of nationalism.[18]

Referring to this in the same essay, Mr. Toynbee suggests two reasons for there being older and deeper causes, and of one of them, the industrial system, this is what he writes:

Industrialism and democracy are elemental forces. In the eighteen-seventies they were still in their infancy, and we cannot yet foresee the ultimate dimensions to which they may grow or forecast the protean shapes which they may assume. What we can now pronounce with certainty is that the European national state —of the dimensions attained by France and Great Britain in the eighteenth century and by Germany and Italy in the nineteenth—is far too small and frail a vessel to contain these forces. The new wines of industrialism and democracy have been poured into old bottles and they have burst the old bottles beyond repair.[19]

This is the problem which Europe has to face. The old bottles, sixteen if you take only the members of the Council of Europe, are no longer adequate; these independent sovereign states are now broken in the economic sense beyond all repair. If the two wines of industrialism and democracy are to be contained in Western Europe, they must be contained in a new barrel large enough to hold not only the wine of one individual state but the wine of all. This means a union of Western Europe including Britain.

Sir Winston Churchill, who has played a large part in directing the attention of people in Europe to the idea of European Union, made the following remarks at a conference in London:

We gaze this morning on the scene of a devasted Europe. The old Europe is divided into twenty or more separate States, each an economic unit fortified by tariff walls and armed with all conceivable weapons to keep out or capture the trade of its neighbours. . . . We have endured and in a broken fashion we have survived the result of this crazy system. There was no hope of recovery if each country simply strove to rebuild itself on the old national lines. We would have to think as Europeans if we were not to be 'paupers or slaves'. The people of Europe would have to sink or swim together and the time had come when they would decide to swim.[20]

Since the rape of Czechoslovakia in 1948 few people have failed to realize the dangers of a divided Europe from the point of view of defence.

M. Spaak is one of those who argue that the defence of Europe demands the unity of Europe, and as defence is urgent, so too is unity. Moreover, without unity it is unlikely that the necessary rearmament programme can be effective, or that each individual state will pull its full weight in the defence of Europe. Not only must we create an efficient united fighting force, but the people must have something positive to fight for, and that something must involve a concept greater than the old national states which in the modern world have little real meaning. If this interpretation is correct then the new concept involves the creation of a political authority, because only with an overriding political authority can the necessary direction and control of a European army be secured. President Eisenhower, who realized that the creation of a European army postulates the creation of a political authority to which it must be responsible, said, 'The establishment of a workable European federation would go far to create confidence among people everywhere that Europe was doing its full and vital share in giving this co-operation.'[21] A strong and united Europe would make a better contribution to the preservation of world peace than a weak and divided one. So long as Europe is divided politically, so long will it be a field for Russian interference. Once it is united the likelihood of successful Communist penetration into Western Europe becomes less. A political union of Europe becomes a major contribution towards the maintenance of world peace.

There are, however, people who have a different theory about the origin of the danger of war. 'Socialists believe,' said the Executive of the British Labour Party, 'that an uncontrolled capitalist economy can function only at the cost of conflicts between nations and classes which may be fatal to civilization in the atomic age.'[22] This statement would sound very well in a leading article in *Pravda*, or as a part of the peroration of one of the speeches which the late Mr. Vyshinsky used to deliver at Lake Success, or as part of the homilies which Mr. Kruschchev delivers at least weekly from the Kremlin or wherever he happens to be. In the good old days the street-corner propagandists liked to use these wild expressions. But from where does the risk of international conflict come today? Is Russia a capitalist and an uncontrolled economy? It may be that in the nineteenth century there was some substance in the general argument that a capitalist economy led to a class conflict and to war. This doctrine, however, must be modified today when all countries, except the Soviet bloc, are primarily capitalist countries. Even though Britain had a Socialist Government for some years her economy is still essentially a capitalist one; for, despite some nationalization and controls, 80 per cent of British and American industry and agriculture is privately owned and controlled. Is it suggested that America came into the two wars of this century because of its 'uncontrolled capitalist economy'? Or that capitalism was the prime cause of the First and Second World Wars? These broke out primarily owing to the anarchy which resulted from a politically divided Europe.

To argue that a capitalist economy is the sole cause of war, is to blind ourselves to the lessons of this century. Not the only cause of war, but the chief one, has been the retention of national sovereignty. The insistence on national sovereignty has not only stood in the way of collective security against aggression being effective, but it has created in many countries that economic insecurity on which dictatorships thrive. Insistence on state sovereignty is the principal cause of the evils of our modern world, for, as Lord Lothian said twentyfive years ago: 'It is the principal cause of economic nationalism and its inevitable consequences, poverty, and unemployment. . . . It is the principal cause of that ending of liberty and democracy and steady extension of state dictatorship which has been the most distressing phenomenon of the last ten years.'[23] The unemployment in Germany in the early 'thirties is generally regarded as having produced Hitler; and the factors which led to unemployment in Germany could not have been removed by the German Government alone. In the United States the central government was able to create a federal Tennessee Valley Authority which, though it interfered with the authority of five states, gave employment to large numbers of people. If, between the wars, there had been in Europe a central political authority as there was in the United States, then perhaps a D.V.A.—a Danube Valley Authority—could have been created in order to provide employment in Central Europe, and such an authority might have prevented the rise of Hitler altogether. The integration of Western Europe, not only in military defence but also in economic organization, is the best safeguard against aggression.

Many people still wonder what are the reasons for Europe's present economic weakness. Why is it that Europe is poor while the United States is rich? Why has Europe been so dependent upon the United States? Why is it that America has been able to increase her productive capacity during the last fifty years so that it is now greater than that of all the rest of the world put together? Why has the same development in productivity not taken place in the continent of Europe, where there are more people than in the United States, and many of them just as skilled? The anwer is to be found in the substantial contrast in political organization. In Western Europe there is a political disintegration not to be found in the United States. In the United States there is one authority—the federal government—controlling those departments of administration which affect the economy as a whole, in comparison with sixteen or more in Europe. In the United States there is one currency, and not sixteen as in Europe. Within the United States there are no trade barriers, such as exist in Europe, which make trading between the states difficult if not impossible. In the United States there is only one market—a large market—and not sixteen. And in consequence, the United States has had the benefits of the second industrial revolution—mass production and standardization—which national sovereignty and political diversity have prevented Europe from enjoying in the same way.

Mr. Paul Hoffman, at the conclusion of his period as Administrator for E.C.A. in Europe, expressed a definite opinion that European recovery and independence of the United States was entirely a matter for the Europeans themselves, and could be achieved if they would scrap their national boundaries and create one market for Western Europe, including Britain. He pointed out that in 1950 the United States with a population of 150 million people had produced $260 billion worth of goods, whereas Western Europe with nearly twice the population, 280 million, had produced barely half as much—$160 billion worth of goods, and that if they produced at the same rate as the United States they would have produced $480 billion worth of goods. Moreover, he thought this could be achieved within five years if effective steps for economic integration and unity were taken at once. What economic integration means was explained by Mr. Hoffman in the following words:

If you look back to 1900 you'll find that your output per man-hour in Europe . . . in Great Britain rather, was about the same as our output per man-hour in the United States. Today our output is almost—per man-hour—is almost two and a half times what it is in Great Britain. That isn't because we're smarter people—we do have perhaps more natural resources: but the primary reason is because while—whereas in Europe you have your 270 million good people divided into twenty tight little compartments, our 150 million people are not divided into compartments—we have forty-eight States but trade and people move freely across State lines—it's no—those State lines are no barrier at all.

Each of the reports of the Anglo-American Productivity Commission when commenting on the increased production per man-hour in the United States as compared with Great Britain shows that it is due to the large free market in the United States; to the increased demand which follows from it; and to the greater use of machinery which is, of course, justified because of the large demand. The creation of a market of 280 million people in Western Europe would, in time, bring about the same results there; and it is only in this way that the section of British industry which is privately owned—the 80 per cent section—can become efficient and increase its production. Far from an economic union creating a protected high-cost European market, a large market should lead to a reduction in the present costs of production. In fact a large home market is a necessary condition for success in the export trade. If manufacturers in Great Britain are making things for a small market in small numbers, they cannot get their prices down; but if they are making them in big quantities for large markets, down their prices will come; and so it will be more possible for them to compete in the export markets of the world.

Britain and the states of Western Europe are living in a changing world which requires of them a complete change in their way of life. The United States and the Soviet Union—each one state, not many—have shown that the way to prosperity and strength lies in a political union in an attempt to become self-supporting. Western Europe (including Britain) as one unit and not twenty different states must follow suit. For an approach to self-sufficiency by Western Europe will mean a considerable increase in agricultural production, which is quite possible; the reduction of imports from non-European countries; and a change in the make-up of the industrial production of Europe so that it can satisfy more of the requirements of the European market than it has in the past. Each of these steps entails economic and political changes. If Europe is to increase her industrial and agricultural production, as she must, and if she is to secure anything like the production per man-hour of the United States, then the trade barriers which exist in Europe must be broken down and a large market and free trading area created. Mass production and standardization must also be introduced. Capital equipment must be increased in many industries and the present wasteful and unnecessary investment which has resulted from Europe being divided into twenty independent states· brought to an end. Increased production and greater efficiency in production will only result from the removal of barriers, the introduction of a common currency in Europe, the abolition of all systems of licensing and quotas and the free movement of populations. But these changes involve political decisions and the creation of a European political authority. Such a political authority exists in the Soviet Union and in the United States; and, as we shall see, such an authority must exist in Western Europe if it is to survive and play a proper part in the future development of civilization as a whole.

What is required is a general realization that the question of European unity is a political question; that the solution to some of Europe's problems will be found only within a European political framework of some kind; and that we can hope for real economic and social progress in Europe only if there is a political authority with power to bring it about. No economic problem in Western Europe today can be solved properly without some kind of political act. The creation of O.E.E.C. was a political step and took a political form. Likewise, the European Payments Union, which had only an economic aim, had to be dressed in political clothes before it was effective. For economic problems are not the key to political problems. It is the other way round. Mr. Lionel Curtis has pointed out that this is the lesson of 1787 in the United States and of 1910 in South Africa. 'Political problems,' he writes, 'with all their thorns must be firmly grasped and settled before we can hope to deal with the social and economic problems.' And the problems of government both in the United States and South Africa were only solved, not by the functional approach, 'a creeping and incipient union which presently arouses an insuperable jealousy', but by a practical solution.

We are living in a revolutionary age. The evidence of it is the thirty years' war from 1914–45, the economic crisis of 1929–38, and the 'cold war' and the recurring economic crises from 1945–59. On the continent of Europe a number of changes in economic organization have taken place which people have not realized: the decline in Europe's share of world manufacturing production; the decline in her share of world trade; the development of tariff barriers between the nations; and an autarchic economy in each which, with the help of Marshall Aid, has intensified the process. Though these changes were brought about in order to provide increased employment and economic stability, they have worked the other way, and undermined both the economic and political institutions of the different countries who developed them. Twenty separate and unco-ordinated governments of countries that are contiguous to one another, each with its separate tariff, taxation, quotas, licences, defence forces, ambassadors, coinage and currency system (all the attributes of a national state), are out of date in Europe in the middle of the twentieth century.

Comparison is often made between the United States and Great Britain with regard to resources. This comparison, of course, is not a fair one, because we are not comparing like with like. The true comparison is between the United States and the states of Western Europe, Great Britain included. If a list of the main raw materials of the world, about fifty, is made up, it will be found that Europe with her associated overseas territories has a greater quantity of raw materials than the United States in all except two—cotton and oil. But at the present time the resources of Western Europe and of Britain are not being utilized to their fullest extent. Professor Tawney emphasized this point in his lecture on *The Western Political Tradition*, when he wrote:

When the present century opened, the Industrial Revolution had re-fashioned the framework of life in Western and central Europe, but was still young and feeble in the agrarian east. Today it has woven the whole continent into one web. Thus political development has gone one way, and economic development another. Interdependence has increased, but so also have frontiers. The multiplication of separate units, each with its own interests and policies, has coincided with a movement towards economic unification, and has contributed to neutralize the benefits promised by it. In such circumstances, the view which sees in the last great breakdown the sole cause of the present miseries of Europe, and of its relative decline vis-à-vis other continents, is less than half the truth. In reality, that decline is not a thing of yesterday. Neither the natural resources of

Europe as a whole, nor its tradition of craftsmanship, nor its ability to harness science to the service of production, compares too unfavourably with those of the United States. If, for twenty years before 1939, it bridged the gap between its imports and exports only with the aid of unrepaid American advances, not the sole explanation, but the single most important one, must be sought in a contrast of political organization. It consists in a failure to make the most of its endowments which has its source in an internal disintegration not yet overcome. . . .

An integration of Europe, whatever its precise form, which broadened the basis of her economy, eliminated customs barriers and competing currencies, and enabled the basic industries of food, fuel, iron and steel, and engineering to be organized to serve a market of two hundred million persons would unquestionably be followed by a general increase in economic prosperity and political strength; but the particular sacrifices and temporary embarrassments entailed by it would not be a trifle.

Those two paragraphs contain the essence of this argument. The weakness and the poverty of Europe result not from any innate weakness in Europe as such or in its peoples or in its resources or in its possibilities for development. They result from a failure to make the most of its endowments. They result from a failure to create a political authority for Western Europe, as the thirteen states of America did at the end of the eighteenth century. They result from the fact that the economic nationalisms of twenty different states make it impossible for there to be a proper economic development of that area as a whole. So long as people continue to think in terms of independent sovereign states and the division of the world as it was in the nineteenth century, then no contribution will be made to the solution of Great Britain's predicament. A new science of politics is required for a new age. In the second half of the twentieth century democracy must be extended over larger areas. Political authorities must be created over areas of territory and population and resources which, because of their size, make it possible for a balanced agricultural and industrial production to take place. There is no reason why the people of Europe, particularly those of France, Italy, Western Germany, Scandinavia and Britain, cannot provide themselves with all the meat they require, all the eggs they require, all the pigs they require, and in fact all the food they require, with perhaps some importation from their overseas territories of wheat—though it must be remembered that France before the war produced more wheat than Canada and is one of the main wheat-exporting countries in the world. So long as we think in terms of one section of the world producing foodstuffs and another not, then we will continue to stagger from one crisis to another.

The previous chapter has shown the mess into which European relations have fallen not only by the creation of so many different institutions but because of the need for the creation of one European authority to handle certain matters which has yet to be realized. The fact that the Little Six have had to go on their own because the other European countries would not go with them indicates the problem which has to be tackled. Yet we cannot work out the basis for the proper form of European organization until the member countries concerned, and that means Britain and the Scandinavian countries as well as France and Germany, are prepared to give serious attention to the problem of bridging the gap between the Little Six and the sixteen. There are a number of problems which must be faced, such as the reappearance in a major way, economically and militarily, of Western Germany; the need for the maintenance of special relations between France and the new French community in Africa, if those relations can be established on a proper basis; the facing of the changed relationship between Britain and the Commonwealth together with an association between them which can be beneficial to both. Moreover, there is need for the establishment of a new kind of relationship between Europe and North America based on a recognition of the fact that the post-war dollar problem is no longer with us; that the N.A.T.O. form of organization, in which one partner is so much the dominating partner, is inadequate; and that any satisfactory relationship must be between Western Europe, including Britain on the one hand, and the United States on the other.

While the European Payments Union existed, and it has been brought to an end more by the actions of Great Britain than any other country, it was more than a geographical concept; it was both a financial and economic one. This today is no longer the case, and, what is worse, some of the member countries concerned are in the process of reducing barriers between themselves and, in consequence, erecting barriers between themselves and the other European countries. The establishment of the European Free Trade Association of the Outer Seven is a very good example of this development, and how wrong a development it is. Nevertheless, if Europe is to be more than a geographical expression, it can only be so if we make it a political reality, and we can only make it a political reality by the major powers, Britain, France, Italy and Germany, being prepared to give way and to come together in an integrated and united organization. Any European organization must have the wholehearted support of the French, the Germans and the British to make it effective. Obviously, this is a long and difficult task, perhaps not to be solved overnight and certainly not by minor and tinkering changes in the present arrangements.

A fundamental re-thinking of attitudes is needed on the part of all our governments but particularly on the part of the British Government. If the British Government would give a lead in the re-thinking by joining the Common Market and then, having made that gesture, working out the simplification of the existing institutions within the Council of

Europe, real progress could be made. We who have the interests of Europe at heart must see to it that this re-thinking begins as soon as possible, for, by drifting, as we are drifting now, we will lose altogether the cohesion which the difficulties of the post-war world forced upon us. We will not have wasted the last ten years if, as a result of the mistakes that have been made, we are now able to simplify the institutions and, with the recognition of the claims of the different groups of Western Europe, to create an organization which will really bring them all together.

This is the challenge which confronts the British people and the British Government today. It is a challenge which has confronted them for nearly twenty years. No country could have risen to greater heights than Britain in 1940 which was the period of her finest hour in the Second World War; but the tragedy is that, having done so well in resisting aggression, we have fallen down so badly in the post-war period by refusing to make any adequate constructive effort to organize a political authority for Europe, of a kind which the second half of the twentieth century requires. So far, our politicians and civil servants have completely failed their own and future generations. Can we hope for a change over the next few years so that we can recover the time that has been wasted? For that is the challenge to Britain today!!

Notes

CHAPTER 1

1 Sir John Wheeler-Bennett, *The Nemesis of Power*, pp. 7–8.
2 R. H. S. Crossman, M.P., *The Listener*, 13th January 1949.
3 *Challenge to Britain*. A programme of action for the next Labour Government. Published by the Labour Party, December 1953.
4 Aneurin Bevan, *In Place of Fear*, p. 170.
5 Aneurin Bevan, *In Place of Fear*, p. 171.

CHAPTER 2

1 Arnold J. Toynbee, *The World after the Peace Conference*, pp. 4 and 13.
2 R. H. Tawney, *The Western Political Tradition*, p. 22.
3 Bertrand de Jouvenel, *Manchester Guardian*, 1954.
4–5 The *Economist Intelligence Unit*.
6–9 Colin Clark, *Manchester Guardian*, 1954.
10 W. A. Lewis, *District Bank Review*, No. 99, September 1951, 'Food and Raw Materials', p. 1, brought up to date for 1958.
11 The *Economist Intelligence Unit*.
12–15 The *Economist Intelligence Unit*.

CHAPTER 3

1 Paper prepared for the author by the *Economist Intelligence Unit*.
2 *Commonwealth Trade*, 1953, p. 1, brought up to date by the *Economist Intelligence Unit*.
3–4 The *Economist Intelligence Unit*.
5 A. R. Conan, *Capital Imports into Sterling Countries*, pp. 52, 85, and *The Economist Intelligence Unit*.
6 Sir J. R. Seeley, *The Expansion of England*, p. 19.
7 *British Security Report*, by a Chatham House Study Group, 1946, p. 76.
8 Lionel Curtis, *The Observer*.
9–11 The *Economist Intelligence Unit*.
12 Leonard Barnes, *Empire or Democracy*, p. 15.
13 Mohamed Zafrullah Khan, speech quoted in the *New York Herald Tribune*.
14 Quoted by H. J. Laski, *Communism*, p. 82.
15 Quoted from a letter to the *Manchester Guardian*, 1954.

16 William O. Douglas, *Strange Lands and Friendly Peoples*, foreword.

17 W. K. Hancock, *Survey of British Commonwealth Affairs*, Vol. 1, p. 487.

CHAPTER 4

1 R. H. Tawney, *The Western Political Tradition*, p. 22.

2 *The Federalist*. Edited by Henry Cabot Lodge, 1888. Essay No. 6, p. 26.

3 John Foster Dulles' speech in London, 1943.

CHAPTER 5

1 A. H. Robertson, *European Institutions*, published by Stevens and Sons Ltd., 1959.

2 *Ibid.*, p. 6.

3 *Ibid.*, p. 79.

4 *Ibid.*, p. 256.

5 *Ibid.*, p. 272.

6 *Ibid.*, pp. 144 and 238.

7 *Ibid.*, pp. 164–8.

8 Key to table showing membership of European Organisations:

(1) Canada and the U.S.A. are Associated members of O.E.E.C. Yugoslavia is represented by an observer.

(2) Canada and the U.S.A. are also members of N.A.T.O.

(3) Yugoslavia is represented by an observer at the E.C.A.C.

(4) The following are also members of the Customs Co-operation Council: Haiti, Indonesia, Israel, Pakistan, and the United Arab Republic.

(5) The U.S.A. is also a member of the Rhine Commission.

9 *Ibid.*, p. 219.

10 *Ibid.*, p. 268.

11 *Ibid.*, p. 230

12 *Official Report of Debates*, 1957, Vol. 1, p. 104, quoted by A. H. Robertson, p. 230.

13 *Ibid.*, p. 166, also quoted by A. H. Robertson, p. 230.

14 Lord Strang, *Home and Abroad*, 1956, p. 280.

14A *Hansard*, Vol. 446, No. 47, col. 397/398.

15 Lord Attlee, *As It Happened*.

16 *Official Report of Debates*, 1951, Vol. 4, pp. 512–16.

17 *Hansard*, Vol. 476, No. 66, Col. 1,935.

18 *Ibid.*, Vol. 476, No. 66, col. 1,949.

19A Notices of Motion, Concession 1955–6, p. 4831.

19B Notices of Motion, Concession 1956–7, p. 704.

20 A. H. Robertson, *European Institutions*, p. 225.

21 Table submitted to the Hague Conference of European Assemblies, 1st–4th April 1959, reprinted as Appendix A to K. Lindsay, *European Assemblies, the experimental period 1949–1959*, Stevens and Sons, Ltd., 1960, pp. 108–9.

CHAPTER 6

1 W. S. Churchill, *Sinews of Peace*, p. 202.

2 *Hansard*, Vol. 480, No. 10, col. 1,403.

3 *European Unity*, by R. W. G. Mackay, Basil Blackwell.

4 *The Times*, 13th January 1951.

5 *Hansard*, 1956, Vol. 561, No. 15, col. 35.

6 Professor J. E. Meade, 'Outside Britain's Market', *Manchester Guardian*, 14th, 15th March 1956.

7 *Treasury Bulletin for Industry*, No. 76 September 1955.

8 *Hansard*, 1956, Vol. 561, No. 15, Cols. 37–8.

9 Quoted in its report on *Britain and the Common Market* by Federal Union, p. 2.

10 Report on *Britain and the Common Market* by Federal Union, p. 3.

11 *Ibid.*, pp. 4–5.

12 *The Economist*, 4th April 1959, pp. 17–19.

13 *The Times*, 11th June 1959.

14 T. Balogh, *New Statesman and Nation*, 'Labour and Trade', 7th February 1959, pp. 177–8.

15–16 *The Economist*, 7th February 1959, 'The European Mettle', p. 471.

17 R. H. Tawney, *Equality*, p. 280.

18 A. J. Toynbee, *Civilization on Trial*, p. 103.

19 A. J. Toynbee, *Civilization on Trial*, pp. 113–14.

20 Speech at European Movement Conference reported in *The Times*, 21st April 1949.

21 *European Movement—Europe.*

22 *European Unity*, Statement of Labour Party, p. 3.

23 Lothian, *Pacifism is not Enough*, p. 55.

A Select Bibliography

ABRAMS, MARK. *Britain and Her Export Trade*, Pilot Press, 1946.

ACTON, LORD. *Lectures in Modern History*, Macmillan & Co. 1921.

AMERICAN MANAGEMENT ASSOCIATION. *The European Common Market*, 1958.

AMERY, RT. HON. L. S. *The Washington Loan Agreements*, MacDonald, 1946.

ANGELL, NORMAN. *For What do we Fight?*, Hamish Hamilton, London, 1939.

ANGELL, NORMAN. *The Steep Places*, Hamish Hamilton, 1947.

ANGLO-RUSSIAN PARLIAMENTARY COMMITTEE (published by) Constitution of the Union of Soviet Socialist Republics (Pamphlet), 1936.

ATTLEE, C. R. *Labour's Peace Aims* (Pamphlet published by the Labour Party), 1939.

BALL, MARGARET. *N.A.T.O. and the European Union Movement*, Stevens & Son Ltd., 1959.

BARNES, LEONARD. *Empire or Democracy?*, Left Book Club, 1939.

BASSETT, R. *The Essentials of Parliamentary Democracy*, Macmillan, 1935.

BEARD, CHARLES AND MARY R. *The Rise of American Civilization*, Jonathan Cape, 1943.

BEARD, CHARLES AND MARY R. *America in Mid-Passage*, Jonathan Cape, 1939.

BELOFF, MAX. *Europe and the Europeans*, Chatto & Windus, 1957.

BLOCH, MARC. *Strange Defeat*, Oxford University Press, 1949.

BOWLE, JOHN. *The Unity of European History*, Jonathan Cape, 1948.

BOYD, ANDREW AND FRANCIS. *Western Union*, U.N.A.'s Guide to European Recovery, Hutchinson, 1948.

BRAILSFORD, H. N. *Why Capitalism Means War*, Victor Gollancz, 1938.

BRAILSFORD, H. N. *Property or Peace?* Victor Gollancz, 1937.

BRIERLY, J. L. *Encirclement*, Oxford Pamphlets on World Affairs, No. 12, 1939.

British Security, a report by a Chatham House Study Group, R.I.I.A., 1946.

BROWN, A. J. *Industrialization and Trade*, Royal Institute of International Affairs, 1943.

BUELL, DEAN, DE WILDE, THOMSON, WERTHEIMER. *New Governments in Europe*, (Revised), Thomas Nelson, New York, 1937.

Bulletin of the Oxford University of Statistics. Basil Blackwell, 1947. Vol. 9, Nos. 3, 4, 7, Vol. 8, No. 10.

Bulletin of the Oxford University of Statistics. Basil Blackwell, 1947. *Studies in War Economics*.

BURNHAM, JAMES. *The Struggle for the World*, John Day, 1947.

BURNS, C. DELISLE. *The First Europe*, George Allen and Unwin, 1947.

CAMPS, MIRIAM. *The Free Trade Area Negotiations*, P.E.P. Occasion Paper, No. 2, 1959.

CARR, EDWARD HALLETT. *The Twenty Years' Crisis, 1919–1939*, Macmillan, 1940.

CARR, EDWARD HALLETT. *Nationalism and After*, Macmillan, 1943.

CARR, EDWARD HALLETT. *Conditions of Peace*, Macmillan, 1942.

CARR, EDWARD HALLETT. *The Soviet Impact on the Western World*, Macmillan, 1947.

CARTER, GWENDOLEN. *The British Commonwealth and International Security*, Ryerson Press, Toronto, 1947.

CLARK, COLIN. *The Conditions of Economic Progress*, Macmillan, 1940.

COLE, G. D. H. *The Intelligent Man's Guide to the Post-war World*, Victor Gollancz, 1947.

COLE, G. D. H. *War Aims, New Statesman* Pamphlet, 1939.

COLE, G. D. H. AND M. I. *The Intelligent Man's Guide to World Chaos*, Victor Gollancz, 1932.

COLE, G. D. H. AND M. I. *The Intelligent Man's Review of Europe Today*, Victor Gollancz, 1933.

COMMISSION REPORT on the Constitution of the Commonwealth of Australia, 1929.

CONDLIFFE, J. B. *The Reconstruction of World Trade*, George Allen and Unwin, 1941.

COUDENHOVE-KALERGI, R. N. *Europe Seeks Unity*, New York, 1948.

CROSSMAN. R H. S. *How We Are Governed*, Left Book Club, 1939.

CURTIS, LIONEL. *Action*, Oxford University Press, 1942.

CURTIS, LIONEL. *Decision*, Oxford University Press, July 1941.

CURTIS, LIONEL. *World Revolution in the Cause of Peace*, Basil Blackwell, Oxford, 1949.

CURTIS, LIONEL. 'A Criterion of Values in International Affairs', Address delivered before the Institute of Politics, Williamstown, Mass., 8th August, 1922 (International Conciliation, No. 183, February 1923).

DAVIES, ERNEST. *'National' Capitalism*, Left Book Club, 1939.

DE MADARIAGA, S. *Anarchy or Hierarchy*, George Allen and Unwin, 1937.

DEAN, VERA MICHELES. *Why Europe went to War*, World Affairs Pamphlet, 1939.

DOBB, MAURICE. *Studies in the Development of Capitalism*, George Routledge, 1946.

DURBIN, E. F. M. *The Politics of Democratic Socialism*, Labour Book Service, 1940.

ECONOMIST INTELLIGENCE UNIT. *Britain and Europe*, 1957.

EUROPEAN INDUSTRIAL CONFERENCE. Full Report, 1958.

EUROPEAN MOVEMENT. *Europe Unites—The Hague Congress and After*, Hollis and Carter, 1949.

FEDERAL UNION. *Britain in the Common Market*, 1959.

FELLNER, WILLIAM J. *Monetary Policies and Full Employment*, University of California Press, 1947.

FISHER, A. G. B. *International Implications of Full Employment in Great Britain*, Royal Institute of International Affairs, 1946.

FISHER, A. G. B. *Clash of Progress and Security*, Macmillan, 1945.

FISHER, A. G. B. *Economic Self-Sufficiency*, Oxford Pamphlets on World Affairs, No. 4.

FISHER, H. A. L. *A History of Europe*, Vols. 1 to 3, Edward Arnold, 1943.

FRY, VARIAN. *The Peace that Failed*, Headline Books published by the Foreign Policy Association, 1939.

GAITSKELL, HUGH. *The Challenge of Co-Existence*, Methuen, 1957.

GALBRAITH, JOHN. *The Affluent Society*, Hamish Hamilton, 1958.

GATHORNE-HARDY, G. M. *The Fourteen Points and the Treaty of Versailles*, Oxford Pamphlets on World Affairs, No. 6, 1939.

GAVIN, LIEUT.-GENERAL JAMES. *War and Peace in the Space Age*, Hutchinson, 1958.

HAAS, ERNEST B. *The Unity of Europe*, Stevens, 1958.

HAINES, E. GROVE. *European Integration*, Johns Hopkins Press, 1957.

HAMILTON, ALEXANDER. *The Federalist*, edited by H. C. Lodge, published by T. Fisher Unwin, 1888.

HAMMOND, J. L. 'Western Civilization' (Article in the *Political Quarterly*, October–December 1939, Vol. 10, No. 4).

HANCOCK, W. K. *Survey of British Commonwealth Affairs*, Vols. 1–3, Oxford University Press, 1940.

HANSEN, ALVIN H. *America's Role in the World Economy*, W. W. Norton Inc., 1945.

HARRIS, SEYMOUR. *The European Recovery Program*, Harvard University Press, 1948.

HARROD, ROY. *Are These Hardships Necessary?*, Rupert Hart-Davis, 1947.

HAWGOOD, JOHN A. *Modern Constitutions since 1787*, Macmillan, 1939.

HAWTREY, R. G. *Western European Union*, Royal Institute of International Affairs, 1949.

HENDERSON, H. D. *Colonies and Raw Materials*, Oxford Pamphlets on World Affairs, No. 7. 1939.

H.M.S.O. *A European Free Trade Area* (Command Paper 72), 1957.

H.M.S.O. *Negotiations for a European Free Trade Area* (Command Papers 648 and 641), 1959.

HILL, CHRISTOPHER. *Lenin and the Russian Revolution*, English University Press, 1947.

HOBSON, J. A. *Imperialism*, George Allen and Unwin, 1938.

HODSON, H. V. *British Security*, a Report of the Royal Institute of International Affairs, 1946.

HORRABIN, J. F. *An Atlas of Empire*, Victor Gollancz, 1937.

HORRABIN, J. F. *An Atlas of Current Affairs*, Left Book Club, 1936.

HORRABIN, J. F. *An Atlas of Post-war Problems*, Penguin Books, 1943.

HUXLEY, JULIAN. *'Race' in Europe*, Oxford Pamphlets on World Affairs, No. 5, 1939.

JENNINGS, W. IVOR. *A Federation of Western Europe*, Cambridge Press, 1940.

KEETON, PROF. GEORGE W. *National Sovereignty and International Order*. A New Commonwealth Institute Monograph, Peace Book Company, 1939.

KING-HALL, SIR STEPHEN. *Defence in the Nuclear Age*, Victor Gollancz, 1958.

KISSINGER, HENRY A. *Nuclear Weapons and Foreign Policy*, Harper, New York, 1957.

KUCZYNSKI, R. R. *'Living Space' and Population Problems*, Oxford Pamphlets on World Affairs, No. 8, 1939.

LABOUR PARTY. *Report of the Forty-second Annual Conference of the Labour Party*, London, 1943.

LASKI, HAROLD J. *What is Democracy?*, The National Peace Council, 1943.

LASKI, HAROLD J. *Authority in the Modern State*, Oxford University Press, 1927.

LASKI, HAROLD J. *The Danger of being a Gentleman*, George Allen and Unwin, 1939.

LASKI, HAROLD J. *The Foundations of Sovereignty and other Essays*, George Allen and Unwin, 1921.

LASKI, HAROLD J. *Liberty in the Modern State*, Penguin Books, 1939.

LASKI, HAROLD J. *The State in Theory and Practice*, George Allen and Unwin, 1935.

LASKI, HAROLD J. *Studies in the Problem of Sovereignty*, Oxford University Press, 1917.

LAYTON, SIR WALTER. *Allied War Aims*, News Chronicle Publication, 1939.

LEAGUE OF NATIONS. *Raw Materials and Problems and Policies*, Economic and Transit Department, 1946.

LENIN, V. I. *Imperialism*, Lawrence and Wishart, 1940.

LIEPMANN, H. *Tariff Levels and the Economic Unity of Europe*, George Allen and Unwin, 1938.

LINDSAY, A. D. *Christianity and Economics*, Macmillan & Co. Ltd., 1933.

LINDSAY, A. D. *The Essentials of Democracy*, Oxford University Press, 1930.

LINDSAY, KENNETH. *Towards a European Parliament*, Strasbourg, 1958.

LIPPMAN, WALTER. *The Communist World and Ours*, Hamish Hamilton, 1959.

LIPPMAN, WALTER. *U.S. Foreign Policy*, Hamish Hamilton, 1943.

Lloyds Bank Review, October 1947.

LOTHIAN, LORD. *The Ending of Armageddon*, published by Federal Union, 1939.

LOTHIAN, LORD. *Pacifism is not Enough (nor Patriotism Either)*, Oxford University Press, 1935.

MACARTNEY, C. A. *National States and Minorities*, Oxford University Press, 1934.

MACKAY, R. W. G. *Coupon or Free?*, Secker and Warburg, 1943.

MACMURRAY, JOHN. *Freedom in the Modern World*, Faber and Faber, 1933.

MACMURRAY, JOHN. *Constructive Democracy*, Faber and Faber, 1943.

MARRIS, A. D. *The Close Integration of Western Europe*, Chatham House, 1948.

MASON, EDWARD S. *Controlling World Trade*, McGraw-Hill Book Company Inc., 1946.

MELCHETT, RT. HON. LORD. *Imperial Economic Unity*, George Harrap & Co., 1930.

MOCH, JULES. *Human Folly: To Disarm or Perish*, Victor Gollancz, 1955.

MOLOTOV, V. M. Speeches U.S.S.R. at the New York Session of the U.N.O. General Assembly, October–December 1946, *Soviet News*, 1947.

MOLOTOV, V. M. Speeches at the Paris Peace Conference, July–October 1946, *Soviet News*.

MOLOTOV, V.M. Speeches and Statements at the Moscow Session of the Council of Foreign Ministers, 1947, *Soviet News*, 1947.

MONTE, HILDA. *The Unity of Europe*, Victor Gollancz, 1943.

MUIR, RAMSAY, *How Britain is Governed*, Constable & Co., 1930.

NOEL-BAKER, P. *The Geneva Protocol*, P. S. King, 1925.

NOEL-BAKER, P. *The Arms Race*, Stevens, 1958.

OLIVER, F. S. *Alexander Hamilton*, Macmillan, 1931.

ORD, LEWIS C. *Secrets of Industry*, George Allen and Unwin, 1944.

PATTERSON, ERNEST MINOR. *An Introduction to World Economics*, Macmillan, New York, 1947.

P.E.P. (Political and Economic Planning). *Britain and World Trade*, Report, June 1947.

PIGOU, A. C. *Aspects of British Economic History, 1918–1925*, Macmillan, 1947.

PIGOU, A. C. *Socialism versus Capitalism*, Macmillan, 1937.

PRIESTLEY, J. B. *The Secret Dream*, Turnstile Press, 1946.

REEVES, EMERY. *The Anatomy of Peace*, George Allen and Unwin, 1946.

ROBBINS, LIONEL. *The Economic Causes of War*, Jonathan Cape, 1939.

ROBERTSON, A. H. *The Council of Europe*, Stevens, 1956.

ROBERTSON, A. H. *European Institutions*, Stevens, 1959.

ROOSEVELT, ELLIOTT. *As He Saw It*, Duell, Sloan and Pearce, 1948.

ROOSEVELT, FRANKLIN D. *Nothing to Fear. The Selected Addresses (1932–45)*, edited by B. D. Zevin, Houghton Mifflin, 1946.

ROSTAS, L. *Comparative Productivity in British and American Industry*, National Institute of Economic and Social Research. Published at the Cambridge University Press, 1948.

ROYAL INSTITUTE OF INTERNATIONAL AFFAIRS. *World Production of Raw Materials*, Information Department Papers, No. 18B, 1941.

ROYAL INSTITUTE OF INTERNATIONAL AFFAIRS. *Atlantic Alliance*, 1952.

ROYAL INSTITUTE OF INTERNATIONAL AFFAIRS. *Britain in Western Europe*, 1956.

RUSSELL, RONALD S. *Imperial Preference*, Empire Economic Union, 1947.

SALTER, SIR ARTHUR. *The Framework of an Ordered Society*, Cambridge University Press, 1933.

SCHUMAN, FREDERICK L. *Design for Power*, Alfred A. Knopf, 1942.

SEELEY, SIR J. R. *The Expansion of England*, Macmillan, 1900.

SHONFIELD, ANDREW. *British Economic Policy Since the War*, Penguin Special, 1958.

SOULE, GEORGE. *America's Stake in Britain's Future*, Oxford University Press, 1946.

STALIN, MARSHAL. *War Speeches*, Hutchinson, 1946.

STANLEY, EUGENE. *World Economic Development*, International Labour Office, Montreal, 1944.

STEED, WICKHAM. *Our War Aims*, Secker and Warburg, 1939.

STERNBERG, FRITZ. *Living with Crisis—The Battle against Depression and War*, John Day, 1949.

STRAUSS, E. *Common Sense about the Common Market*, George Allen and Unwin, 1958.

STUDY GROUP. The Royal Institute of International Affairs, *Political and Strategic Interests of the United Kingdom*, Oxford University Press, 1939.

SWEEZY, PAUL M. *The Theory of Capitalist Development*, Dennis Dobson, 1946.

TAWNEY, R. H. *Acquisitive Society*, George Bell, 1921.

TAWNEY, PROF. R. H. *Why Britain Fights*, Macmillan War Pamphlets, No. 13, 1941.

TAWNEY, PROF. R. H. *Harrington's Interpretation of His Age*, from the Proceedings of the British Academy, 1941.

TAWNEY, PROF. R. H. *Equality*, George Allen & Unwin, 1938.

THORNTON, A. P. *The Imperial Idea and its Enemies*, Macmillan, 1959.

TOYNBEE, ARNOLD J. *The World After the Peace Conference*, Oxford University Press, 1926.

TOYNBEE, ARNOLD J. *Studies in History*, Vols. 1–4, Oxford University Press, 1951.

TOYNBEE, ARNOLD J. *Survey of International Affairs*, Oxford University Press, 1934.

TOYNBEE, ARNOLD J. *Civilization on Trial*, Oxford University Press, 1945.

UNITED STATES DEPARTMENT OF COMMERCE. *The United States in the World Economy*, Bureau of Foreign and Domestic Commerce, 1943.

VAN DOREN, CARL. *The Great Rehearsal—The Story of the Making and Ratifying of the Constitution of the United States*, Viking Press, 1948.

VINER, JACOB. *Studies in the Theory of International Trade*, Harper, New York, 1937.

VYSHINSKY, A. Y. Speeches at the Paris Peace Conference, July–October 1946, *Soviet News*, 1946.

WARD, BARBARA. *The West at Bay*, George Allen and Unwin, 1948.

WEBB, SYDNEY AND BEATRICE. *Soviet Communism*, Longmans, Green, 1935.

WELLES, SUMNER. *Where are we Heading?*, Harper, New York, 1946.

WELLS, H. G. *The New World Order*, Secker and Warburg, 1940.

WHEARE, K. C. *Federal Government*, Oxford University Press, 1946. Under the Auspices of the Royal Institute of International Affairs.

WILKIE, WENDELL L. *One World*, Cassell, 1943.

WILLIAMS, SHIRLEY. *The Common Market and its Forerunners*, 1958, Fabian International Bureau.

WOODWARD, E. L., BUTLER AND ROHAN. *Documents on British Foreign Policy, 1919–39*. At the Oxford University Press under the authority of His Majesty's Stationery Office, 1946.

WOOLF, LEONARD. *Barbarians at the Gate.* Left Book Club, 1939.

WOOLF, LEONARD. *Imperialism and Civilization*, Hogarth Press, 1928.

WRIGHT, QUINCY. *Mandates under the League of Nations*, University of Chicago Press, 1930.

ZIFF, WILLIAM B. *Two Worlds*, Harper, New York, 1946.

ZIMMERN, ALFRED. *The Prospects of Civilization*, Oxford Pamphlets on World Affairs, No. 1, 1939.

ZURCHER, ARNOLD J. *The Struggle to Unite Europe, 1940–1958*, New York University Press, 1958.

Index

Index